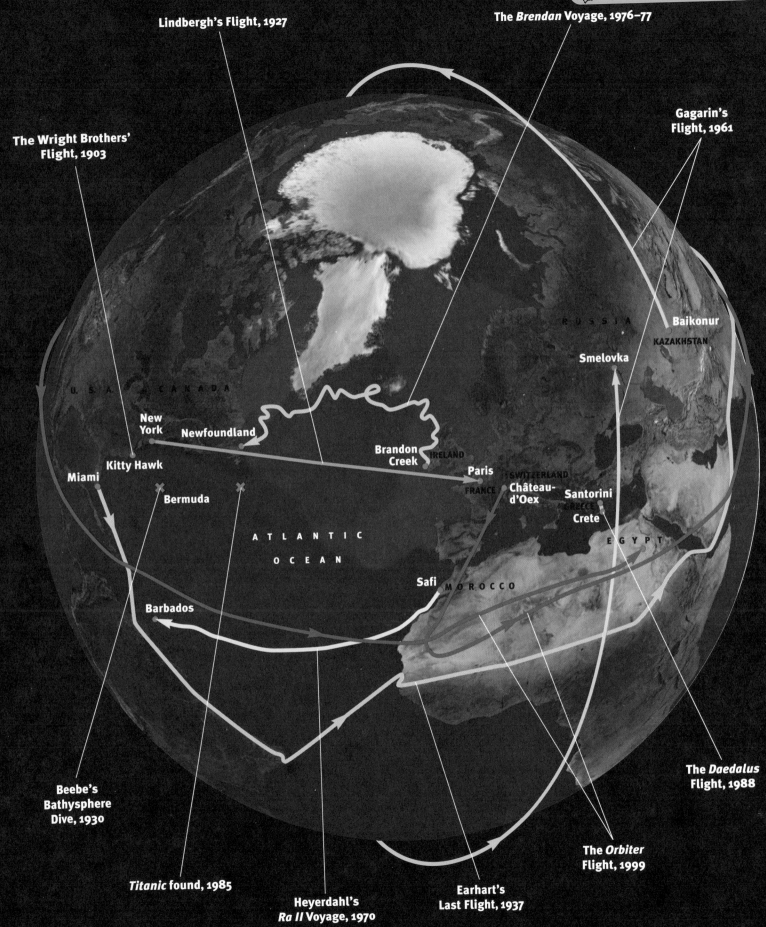

Lindbergh's Flight, 1927

The *Brendan* Voyage, 1976–77

The Wright Brothers' Flight, 1903

Gagarin's Flight, 1961

Baikonur

KAZAKHSTAN

RUSSIA

Smelovka

New York

Newfoundland

Brandon Creek

IRELAND

Kitty Hawk

Paris

SWITZERLAND

Miami

FRANCE

Château-d'Oex

Santorini

Bermuda

GREECE

Crete

EGYPT

ATLANTIC

OCEAN

U.S.A.   CANADA

Safi

MOROCCO

Barbados

The *Daedalus* Flight, 1988

Beebe's Bathysphere Dive, 1930

The *Orbiter* Flight, 1999

Titanic found, 1985

Heyerdahl's *Ra II* Voyage, 1970

Earhart's Last Flight, 1937

LIFE

THE GREATEST
Adventures
OF ALL TIME

LIFE

THE GREATEST
Adventures
OF ALL TIME

WITH A FOREWORD BY WILL STEGER

Brown Brothers

Previous pages: Wilbur Wright brought the brothers' famous *Flyer* to New York City for a demonstration in 1909.
Below: In 1912, a detachment from Robert Falcon Scott's Antarctic expedition scrambled across the breaking ice.

Editors Robert Sullivan, Robert Andreas
Picture Editor Barbara Baker Burrows
Art Director Ian Denning
Senior Writer Catherine Buni
Associate Editors Anne Hollister,
Lela Nargi, Dierdre Van Dyk
Deputy Picture Editor
Christina Lieberman
Associate Picture Editors
Lila Garnett, Suzanne Hodgart
Writer-Reporters Kari Bodnarchuk,
Deb Fleischman, Katharine Wroth
Picture Research Lauren Steel,
Hillevi Loven (Assistant)
Copy Desk Madeleine Edmondson
(Deputy), Kathleen Berger, J.C. Choi,
Joel Griffiths, Larry Nesbitt,
Jerome Rufino, Sékou, Pam Warren

LIFE Books

**Time Inc.
Home Entertainment**

President
Stuart Hotchkiss
**Executive Director,
Branded Businesses**
David Arfine
**Associate Director,
Branded Businesses**
Kenneth Maehlum
**Executive Director,
Marketing Services**
Carol Pittard
Product Manager
Niki Viswanathan
Assistant Product Manager
Michelle Kuhr

**Director, Retail & Special
Sales**
Tom Mifsud
**Manager, Retail & New
Markets**
Bozena Szwagulinski
**Coordinator, Retail
Marketing**
Gina Di Meglio
**Editorial Operations
Director**
John Calvano
**Assistant Editorial
Operations Manager**
Emily Rabin
Book Production Manager
Jessica McGrath
**Associate Book Production
Manager**
Jonathan Polsky

Fulfillment Manager
Richard Perez
**Assistant Fulfillment
Manager**
Tara Schimming
Executive Assistant
Mary Jane Rigoroso

We welcome your
comments and suggestions
about LIFE Books.
Please write to us at:

LIFE Books
Attention: Book Editors
PO Box 11016
Des Moines, IA 50336-
1016

If you would like to order
any of our hardcover
Collector's Edition books,
please call us at
1-800-327-6388
(Monday through Friday,
7:00 a.m.– 8:00 p.m. or
Saturday, 7:00 a.m.–
6:00 p.m. Central Time).

Please visit our Web site at
www.TimeBookstore.com

Copyright 2000
Time Inc. Home
Entertainment

ISBN: 1-929049-06-4
Library of Congress Catalog
Number: 00-101247

The Spirit of Adventure

Foreword by **Will Steger**

In the early '60s a buddy from Minneapolis and I shipped our 20-foot-long folding kayak to Juneau, Alaska. Young, short on cash, we hitchhiked and hopped a ferry to rendezvous with our boat. Our plan was to kayak Alaska's Inside Passage, which turned out to be a wild and dangerous trip. We fought storms and bugs all along the route and paddled among pods of killer whales. When we finally made it to Skagway, we had to portage a 40-mile trail that led to the headwaters of the Yukon River. From there we paddled to the Arctic Circle, where we packed up our boat and hitchhiked back home to Minnesota, just in time to begin another year of college.

It was a fortunate time for adventure because many of the areas we traveled across were marked UNMAPPED. Just big, blank, white spots on the maps. It was in these vast sections of wilderness that we met some of the last remaining men who had moved north for the gold rush of 1898. These old-timers still lived in their log cabins, deep in the wilderness, and were glad for the company of a couple of innocent, weather-beaten young men. I have vivid memories of warming up next to their woodstoves, complaining bitterly about the mosquitoes and listening to their stories about the old days.

This type of adventure was new to me. I was 18 years old, and for most of the trip I was miserable. During the frequent storms on the sea, I feared for my life. I missed home, with its warm, dry bed.

As we shared our complaints with our grizzled hosts, they muttered in reply, "Oh, you'll be back, boys. Mark my words, you'll be back." At the time I would have bet big money they were wrong.

That kayak trip changed my life. A couple of months after we returned home, I found myself ordering more maps and charting a route that would take us 3,000 miles by kayak the following summer, from Jasper, Alberta, all the way to the Arctic Ocean. Then it was trips to the tops of unclimbed mountains and down big-rapid rivers. It was tens of thousands of miles by canoe and dogsled. It was journeys to the North Pole and across the Antarctic continent. Thirty years of it.

Why? This is the question I am most frequently asked. "Why do you adventure?"

It has never been an easy question to answer in anything less than a ramble, since, like describing the beautiful scent of a flower, describing the "why" of adventure must always fall short. It is all in the experiencing. So sometimes I try to duck the question with my own version of "Because it's there." Other times, I try to puzzle it out.

Adventure is natural and obvious to children, and it is rare that I get the "Why" question from anyone younger than 16. (Kids typically want answers to really big questions, like "How do you go to the bathroom when it's 50 below?")

"Why adventure?" is an adult's question. When we grow up, our instinctual, go-for-it sensibility is replaced by an analytical, judgmental one. We grow out of the spontaneity that we knew as children. As a teenager I went looking for adventure. My goals were unclimbed mountains, remote wilderness rivers; there were risks galore and constant excitement. There was a sense of discovery: land I was seeing for the first time, thousands and thousands of miles of trackless, untamed wilderness. I had, as many of us do at that point in our lives, a restless mind, and this beauty slowed me down, and for the first time I was able to live in the moment. All I saw was beauty. Everywhere. In the hushed valleys through which the quiet green rivers flowed, and in the eternal snows of glacial ice caps. I was young, and so I was wide-eyed. If I were trying to explain this, now, to a young person, he or she would say, "Of course."

There is a notion today that, since the highest mountains have all been climbed and the Poles have both been reached, there are no more adventures to

6

be had. I couldn't disagree more. Adventure is in the individual. It is as close as putting on your boots in the morning and heading out the door. And it's not about the prize, the trophy, the goal, the gold. Robert Service in his poem *The Spell of the Yukon* put it perfectly: "Yet it isn't the gold that I'm wanting/so much as just finding the gold." That's adventure—the finding of it.

And that, again, is a young person's attitude; a kid wouldn't know what to do with the gold if he had it. When I went to Alaska at the age of 18 and

met with the old men who, long before, had come to Alaska for gold, I wondered why they had stayed. "You'll be back, boys," they said, perhaps sensing that what had kept them in a wild place such as that—their youthful spirit, their adventuresome spirit—was present in their guests.

After that adventure in the Yukon, I very quickly forgot the miserable times and spent the following year dreaming about repeating the experience. Getting back to a place—a place in the wild, a place in my spirit.

Introduction

Adventure An Attempt at a Definition

O ne can make an argument that the first pure adventurers were those from Africa and Asia who migrated to Europe more than a million years ago. We won't be making that argument in this book, but it could be made. One could say that ancient Indonesians who discovered Australia, or Asians who walked the Alaskan land bridge from Siberia to North America 60,000 years ago, were adventurers. They certainly were adventurous.

We will not deny that when the Norwegian Viking Leif Eriksson sailed to Vinland in the year 1000, thus becoming the first European to discover the New World (unless you buy into the implications of Tim Severin's achievement, as detailed in this book), he had quite an adventure. We will not deny that when Marco Polo traveled the Silk Road at the end of the 13th century, he had many adventures. We will not deny the adventurousness of Christopher Columbus in finding the Caribbean in 1492, or of Vasco Núñez de Balboa in reaching the Pacific in 1513, or of Juan Ponce de León in exploring Florida in the same year. In 1519, Hernando

Cortés was in Mexico while Ferdinand Magellan was heading for Tierra del Fuego—big adventures. From 1577 to 1589, the English were broadly adventuresome as Sir Francis Drake was patrolling the Pacific off California while Sir Walter Raleigh's men cruised off North Carolina. In 1607 the brave, charismatic Capt. John Smith led a group of scared but nonetheless adventurous settlers to Jamestown. Henry Hudson questing in the Arctic, Sir Alexander Mackenzie questing after the Northwest Passage, Lewis and Clark questing all over the American West and Capt. James Cook questing all over the world: great adventurers all.

But adventurers first?

We would argue not. Most were explorers, principally, while others were variously conquistadors, missionaries and mercenaries. Among their reasons for venturing, adventure was low on the list.

The thing is: There were, in bygone ages, places to be discovered, lands to be explored or conquered. Those who might otherwise have adventured, explored. Yes, on paper an explorer may look quite the same as an adventurer. They share several

At the end of the first millennium A.D., Leif Eriksson found a new world (top left), and three centuries later, Marco Polo opened another (above). But were they adventurers?

traits—boldness, stoicism, strength. But the reason for the enterprise is fundamentally different, and an adventurer is, therefore, a very different beast.

Why does he or she go? An explorer has to go because the boss tells him to (or, as in the cases of Isabella with Columbus and Thomas Jefferson with Lewis and Clark, asks politely). A conqueror has to go because power is his currency, and an extension of power makes him richer. A trader such as Polo or Hudson has to go because the largest pot of gold is always at the far end of the rainbow.

Why does an adventurer have to go? (And, oh, yes, an adventurer *has* to go.) What motivates the adventurer?

This is difficult to answer, even for adventurers themselves. America's greatest living adventurer, Will Steger, who drove a dogsled team to the North Pole and another clear across Antarctica, has taken a stab at it in his Foreword to this book, but admits, "It has never been an easy question to answer in anything less than a ramble, since, like describing the beautiful scent of a flower, describing the 'why' of adventure must always fall short. It is all in the

experiencing." In an interview later in the book, the greatest living adventurer from anywhere on the planet, Sir Edmund Hillary, speaks of the "joy" he got from standing on a summit alone but says he would choose to pursue this or that project principally because it provided "a good challenge."

That's part of it, surely: the test. But as Steger's and Hillary's waffling implies, adventure is what's left when cause and reason aren't factored in. Since there is no clear reward besides the doing of the deed itself, an adventure's appeal is abstract. The fuzzy terms "a sense of adventure" and "a spirit of adventure" are apt, for there is something unquantifiable but nonetheless intrinsic in the marrow of an adventurer. An adventurous nature demands: Accept the dare. Take the next step. Onward, upward. There is a spark in the adventurous spirit that won't be extinguished, a thirst never slaked. Death has ended the career of many adventurers, yet one is sure that most of them died without regret and would otherwise have continued on to new adventures the next day.

As we've said and seen, even adventurers strug-

In fourteen hundred and ninety-two, Columbus sailed the ocean blue (and only a year later was celebrated in this woodcut from Giuliano Dati's *Narrative of Columbus*). But was he an adventurer?

In 1522 the *Victoria,* seen in a 16th century line engraving, was the only one of Ferdinand Magellan's five ships to survive the first circumnavigation of the earth. But was Magellan an adventurer?

Everest expedition, whose members Hillary and Tenzing Norgay reached the summit, asked himself a bald question near the end of his book *The Conquest of Everest:* Was it worth it? "It was so beyond doubt," he answered. He talked of the beauty that he and his comrades had seen, the exhilaration they had felt, the mateship they had built. And then he wrote: "Adventure can be found in many spheres, not merely upon a mountain, and not necessarily physical. Ultimately, the justification for climbing Everest, if any justification is needed, will lie in the seeking of other 'Everests' by others, stimulated by this event as we were inspired by others before us . . . The ascent of Everest seems to have stirred the spirit of adventure latent in every human breast."

So it isn't necessarily something necessary, like the finding of America or the opening of China. It's what accomplishing the task means unto itself.

Having said that, in this book we've got a Navy commander piloting a nuclear sub, an anthropologist trying to trace bygone migration routes, a man walking on the moon. These things had to be done, did they not? Yes, certainly. And the two Poles had to be reached, along with the highest and lowest places on earth. But what was the profit of these achievements, beyond bragging rights? Was anyone going to colonize Everest, the Arctic Ocean, the moon? More than a few critics have complained that

gle to put their finger on it, often sounding defensive, if nobly so, when discussing motive. The Englishman George Mallory, who died on Mount Everest in June 1924, famously said of man's need to climb the mountain: "Because it's there." His simple but bottomless phrase resides at a strange intersection of banality and metaphysics, and it has been echoed by other adventurers. Those who succeed gloriously are routinely modest about their achievements and wonder what they have done and why. John Hunt, leader of the triumphant 1953 British

In 1519, Hernando Cortés (third from right, in a contemporaneous Aztec drawing) arrived at Tenochtitlán (now Mexico City). But was he an adventurer?

NASA's star treks represent the biggest waste of money in history. They ask of the Pathfinder probe, for instance: Why in the world go to Mars?

Because it's there.

We are not naive: There were political reasons and implications behind the *Nautilus* sub mission, the space race and other items in this book—even the work of Jacques Cousteau for the French Navy. There were economic rewards for Bob Ballard in finding the *Titanic* and for Charles Lindbergh in finding Paris. How did their efforts differ from Polo's, from Ponce de León's?

Only in balance. You put motive on the scale and see which way it tips. If it tips toward money or power, the adventurer is an explorer. If it tips toward adventure, the explorer is an adventurer.

This is why adventuring is a modern phenomenon, and why the subjects in this book are 20th century heroes. When you looked around a hundred years ago, just about everything that might be found had been found. The great remaining grails were the Poles and Everest, and this is why they inspired the greatest adventures. Their geological or strategic significance was negligible to worthless. A quarter acre in Nevada might be more useful. But Peary, Amundsen, Hillary and Norgay became worldwide icons of extraordinary magnitude. When the roll was called at century's end, they were way up there. For what? For getting there and getting back. And what, today, is the fruit of their achievement? Basically, as this book proves, a whopping good yarn.

Ernest Shackleton, who got back but didn't succeed, understood adventure. In a want ad soliciting compatriots for his dicey 1914 escapade in the Antarctic—"safe return doubtful"—he could offer as payment only "Honour and recognition in case of success." He got his crew, and they were a game and strong crew. He had gone trolling for adventurers and had hooked a number of them.

How many are left, in our high-tech, Polar-tec age? Too few, which is why this book is worth reading. It's why these pictures enthrall.

They did that? For what?

They went there? Why?

Because it was there.

— Robert Sullivan

In 1609, Henry Hudson sailed a river in the *Half Moon*, causing eponymic havoc: The river was named for him, then a school of painting (to which this Albert Bierstadt oil belongs) was named for the river. But was Hudson an adventurer?

Water

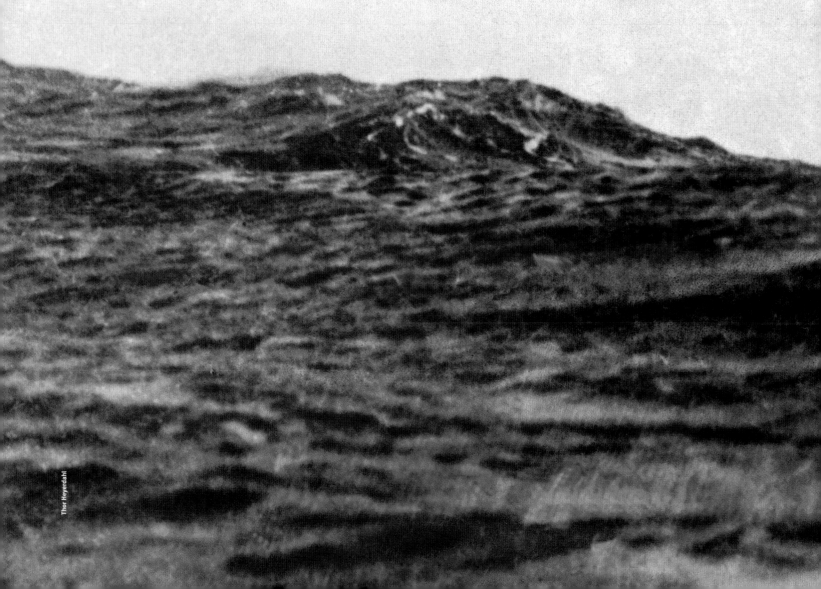

The Voyage of the *Kon-Tiki*,
Pacific Ocean, 1947

The Great Survivor

When **Ernest Shackleton**'s overland expedition failed, he set off on the most daring boat trip ever.

Men Wanted for Hazardous Journey. Small Wages, bitter cold, long months of complete darkness, constant danger, safe return doubtful. Honour and recognition in case of success." According to one tale, perhaps apocryphal, that was the wording of an ad Ernest Shackleton placed to solicit men for his 1914 Imperial Trans-Antarctic Expedition. Not a very enticing offer, but 27 men did sign on, and although they were unsuccessful in the technical sense—before they even set foot on land, their ship was crushed in a vise of ice, marooning them for more than a year—they did manage, miraculously and heroically, a safe return.

Royal Geographical Society (2)

Efforts to free the ship from the ice ended on February 24, 1915, when Shackleton declared *Endurance* a winter station: "The summer had gone," he wrote. "[T]he birds were leaving us. The land showed still in fair weather on the distant horizon, but it was beyond our reach now."

Diversions: To stave off boredom, the men played games (above, Frank Hurley and Leonard Hussey at the chessboard), at times involving their dogs (below, the smallest crewman, Hussey, hoisted Samson). The dogs eventually had to be shot to both conserve and provide food.

Shackleton's expedition has become perhaps the most storied epic of survival. There are more than a dozen books that tell the tale—and it's quite a tale.

Born on Irish ground to English blood in 1874, Shackleton from the first seemed of two worlds. A restless student, he left school at 16 and joined the merchant marine, where, in a turnabout, he gained a reputation as bookish. He would spout the verse of Browning from the decks, and his colleagues viewed him as not a little odd. In 1901 he signed on

for Robert F. Scott's *Discovery* expedition to Antarctica. Six years later he returned on his own. Within 100 miles of the South Pole, their feet split with frostbite, all but starved, Shackleton and his men turned back. They had failed to reach the Pole, although their try had bested Scott's by 360 miles.

Much to Shackleton's dismay, the Norwegian explorer Roald Amundsen conquered the South Pole in 1911. But the loss of that great trophy didn't diminish Shackleton's wanderlust. He had a com-

fortable home (largely financed by his wife Emily's fortune) and three children, but soon he was plotting the first crossing of Antarctica on foot.

According to the plan, two ships would set sail. One, with Shackleton at the helm, would cross the treacherous Weddell Sea and land at Vahsel Bay. A second would travel over the Ross Sea; its crew would land and stash supplies for Shackleton's overland crossing. The challenges were obvious: The Weddell Sea was notorious for relentless and crush-

Exercise: Physical fitness was as important as mental fitness. Skis that were to be used for transport now served for sport. After a schuss, Robert Clark stowed his gear.

ing ice; Vahsel Bay offered no proven landing; and the territory between the Weddell Sea and the Pole was uncharted. Shackleton made his plans with these difficulties in mind, but he couldn't have known that the sea's ice was destined to freeze early and thick that season.

In August 1914, while other Englishmen were mobilizing to do battle in the Great War, the crew of the *Endurance*—a 300-ton Norwegian-built schooner named to reflect Shackleton's family motto (*Fortitudine vincimus,* "By endurance we conquer")—slipped down the Thames and headed south. On December 7, at latitude 57 degrees south, the first ice appeared, and for six weeks the *Endurance* smashed through frozen seas. By January 29, the ice had won, and it held the *Endurance* fast in a gyrating mass of tumbled, jagged slabs—some thrusting 20 feet into the air. The *Endurance* had

Photographer Frank Hurley used the Paget process to shoot in color (opposite) and set some 20 flashes on the ice pack to shoot *Endurance* at night.

sailed 12,000 miles, pushed through pack ice for 1,000 miles more, and now, less than 100 miles from its destination, was trapped. "It was more than tantalising," wrote Dr. Alexander H. Macklin, one of two surgeons on board, "it was maddening."

Shackleton calmly announced that the expedition would winter on the ice until spring, a duration that could extend as long as nine months. He then quickly implemented sanity-saving routines and *passe-temps*. The men amused themselves with impersonations. They raced their 60 or so Canadian sled dogs, wagering chocolate and cigarettes on the contests. Shackleton, wrote Macklin, displayed "real greatness. He did not rage at all, or show out-

wardly the slightest sign of disappointment."

Even when the ship began to crack, Shackleton kept the expedition together, ordering his men to set up "Ocean Camp." Using the *Endurance*'s battered timbers, they built a galley and storehouse on the ice and filled it with three tons of salvaged food. They surrounded this principal building with five linen tents and three lifeboats.

On October 27, 1915, the *Endurance* sank. Shackleton stayed up all night, and the next morning, after serving his crew coffee at five a.m., he announced, "Ship and stores have gone—so now we'll go home."

It would take another half year before they could

Mitchell Library, State Library of New South Wales

Royal Geographical Society

Frank Hurley's Photographic Memoir

For all the journals and narratives left in the wake of Shackleton's adventures, it is perhaps the work of Frank Hurley—who took all the pictures in this chapter—that most vividly tells the story of the *Endurance*. Hurley, who ran away from his Australian home when he was 13, was, according to the ship's chief officer, Lionel Greenstreet, "a warrior with his camera [who] would go anywhere or do anything to get a picture." As the *Endurance* went down, Hurley recorded the tragedy. Much of that record, sadly, is gone: When Shackleton ordered his men to jettison all but vital supplies, Hurley was forced to abandon his gear, saving only a pocket camera. Of more than 500 glass-plate negatives, he was able to preserve only 120. The images from them still haunt, more than fourscore years later.

set off, but home they would eventually go.

On April 9, 1916, the ice finally thinned enough for the men to again take to the sea. Their only hope for survival, Shackleton determined, was to reach Elephant Island, some 100 miles away. After seven days of storm and cold, having to bail their open lifeboats constantly, the men arrived—some of them just barely alive.

Shackleton knew that to stay on the remote outpost, several hundred miles from the southernmost tip of South America, almost certainly meant death. So he and five volunteers took to the sea again in the 22.5-foot *James Caird,* largest of the lifeboats. Their goal: the whaling camps off South Georgia Island, some 800 miles north.

In what is now widely regarded as the most remarkable boat journey of all time, the men spent 17 days on the planet's stormiest ocean. Shackleton biographer Roland Huntford has described the *Caird*

On October 19, 1915, Shackleton surveyed his damaged ship, which would go under eight days later. The men hauled three lifeboats, including the *James Caird* (above), to Ocean Camp, which was on an ice floe that began to break up in spring. They then moved to Patience Camp, where Hurley (left) and Shackleton pitched a tent.

Hurley recorded the departure of the *Caird* (above and below), though he would doctor the latter image and name it *The Rescue*, implying it showed Shackleton's heroic return. The men who had been left behind were hardly this hale when the *Yelcho* arrived to save them.

as "a cockleshell that was like an insect swimming in a tidal wave." Expedition member Frank Worsley, an expert navigator, took only four sextant readings along the way. Had his calculations been wrong by one degree, the *Caird* would have sailed off course. But the boat plunged straight on, through snow, hurricane-force wind and seas as high as 20 feet. The men pulled screws from the *Caird* and forced them into the soles of their boots for traction. Emaciated, they reached land, then had to trek 22 miles over the unmapped, glacier-draped mountains of South Georgia to reach the whaling port. As they began their 36-hour hike, Shackleton said, "If anything happens to me while those fellows are waiting for me, I shall feel like a murderer."

It never came to that. Four months later, after three unsuccessful attempts to sail back in rescue, Shackleton returned to his crew. They were scratching limpets from the shore when he arrived; even the penguins had abandoned desolate Elephant Island. Near-starved, the men had endured by huddling under their lifeboats, singing songs to hold on

to the last threads of hope and sanity. All 28 men who sailed on the *Endurance* survived. As for Sir Ernest, he would live only a few years more: He died of a heart attack on South Georgia in 1922 while commanding yet another Antarctic expedition.

Years later, Raymond Priestley, who had served as the geologist on Shackleton's 1907 Antarctic expedition, reflected: "For swift and efficient travel, give me Amundsen; for scientific investigation, give me Scott; but when you are at your wits' end and all else fails, go down on your knees and pray for Shackleton."

Royal Geographical Society (4)

The 22 men of Elephant Island would endure four terrible months, but all would be saved. Their camp was now reduced to a single construct (right) made from the remaining two lifeboats, overturned, with cloth from the tents draped as walls.

A Man of Depth

Jules Verne imagined a weird undersea realm. **William Beebe** visited that place.

On a barge off the coast of Bermuda, Gloria Hollister listened for a voice, her pen poised to record whatever words came through her headset. Finally, she heard William Beebe speak: "Only dead men have sunk below this."

It was June 1930. Six hundred feet below the barge, Beebe and engineer Otis Barton were dangling in a 5,000-pound, 4.5-foot-wide steel bubble. Their "bathysphere"—from the Greek *bathys,* or "deep"—had taken them to a place no living person had been. For all the two men knew at that moment, their metal cocoon, under thousands of pounds of pressure, might fail, and, as Beebe later wrote,

After Beebe had climbed through the portal, 10 huge nuts sealed a 400-pound door. Then the sphere was hoisted from the ship, a former British man-of-war, and dropped into the sea.

In 1932 teammates Barton (left) and Beebe posed beside the record-setting bathysphere before making a dive off the coast of Bermuda.

"unthinkably instant death would result from the least fracture of glass or collapse of metal. There was no possible chance of being drowned, for the first few drops would have shot through flesh and bone like steel bullets."

Danger for the sake of science was nothing new to Beebe, who, after an upbringing in Brooklyn, would tramp the world's wilds as the New York Zoological Gardens' curator of birds and, later, the Zoological Society's director of tropical research. During more than 30 bathysphere descents—from that first endeavor to a subsequent deep-sea record of 3,028 feet, set in 1934—he put fear aside and spent hours peering out the fused-quartz window while his partner, Barton, tended to the oxygen system, thermometer and other equipment. Beebe's recorded sightings—"exploding" scarlet shrimp, flying mollusks, sea dragons—were met with skepticism in his day. "But the miracle," says marine biologist and deep-sea diver Sylvia Earle, who counts Beebe as an influence, "is that he came as close as he did."

Charles William Beebe—renowned biologist and writer, intrepid adventurer—died at age 84 in 1962 in a suitable locale: the Simla Research Station near Arima, Trinidad.

Sylvia Earle Asks, "How Low Can You Go?"

The third time was the charm for marine biologist Sylvia Earle in 1979. Twice already, Earle had clambered into the 1,000-pound "Jim" suit (named for the first to test it in the 1920s, diver Jim Jarrett) and begun her descent. Twice already, her communications wire had snapped and she had been forced to resurface. Now, strapped to a metal platform welded onto the front of a submarine, the 43-year-old aquanaut went down a third time, hoping to set a new depth record for an untethered solo dive. The sub landed at 1,250 feet and discharged Earle. The record was hers instantly, but she spent two and a half hours face-to-fin with scores of luminescent sea dwellers.

Today, as explorer-in-residence at the National Geographic Society, Earle still dives—and spends the rest of her time writing and lecturing, hoping to combat the public's "profound complacency" about the earth's last frontier.

Earle was the first to don the inner-space Jim suit for open-sea exploration. A minisub served as her taxi to the depths (opposite).

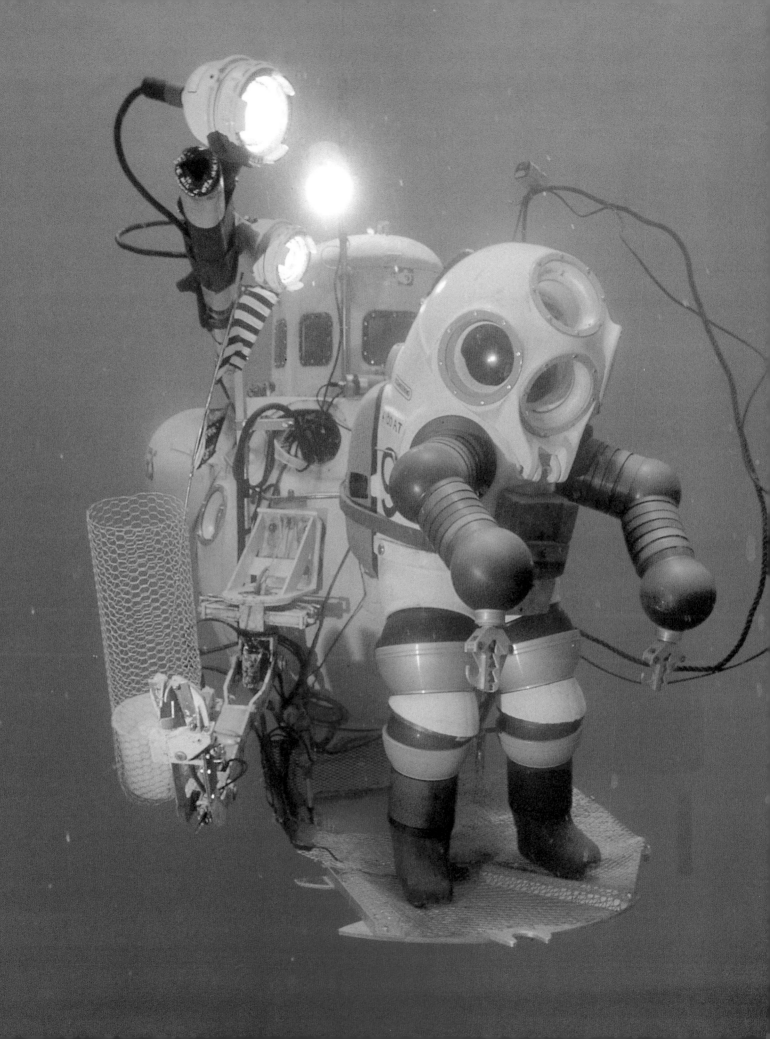

The Manfish

The undersea world of **Jacques Cousteau** was a colorful, poetic, magical place.

Tom Williamson

I hate danger," the Frenchman Jacques-Yves Cousteau once said. How to credit such a remark from a man who plunged below the ocean's surface more than 30,000 times, free-diving to depths of 300 feet? Fifty fathoms down: an unlikely spot to find a man who suffered chronic anemia as a child and remained thin and wiry for 87 years. But as much as he might have hated danger, he loved the sea—particularly the undersea. "From birth," Cousteau wrote, "man carries the

As a scientist and inventor he might have stayed anonymous, but by taking his movie camera to the depths (right), Cousteau became world famous.

Joe Thompson

Cousteau was forever testing new garb and equipment. His 1953 diving suit (above) was a modified version of the one he wore in 1950 when he was assisted by diver Terry Young (at left) during Aqua-Lung trials off San Pedro, Calif.—trials disrupted at one point by a shark.

Popperfoto

Tom Williamson

weight of gravity on his shoulders . . . But man has only to sink beneath the surface and he is free. Buoyed by water, he can fly in any direction—up, down, sideways—by merely flipping his hand. Underwater, man becomes an archangel."

Above water, Cousteau was a sainted figure to the millions who watched his wondrous films and television shows, and, particularly, to other divers. Man had wanted to dive forever: The ancient Assyrians imagined breathing underwater, depicting people sucking air from goatskin bellows. In the 19th and early 20th century, divers breathed oxygen pumped from above; it was a perilous business, as tubes could snap, severing the lifeline. By the 1930s, compressed air was brought below, but an inefficient hand-operated valve system, among other shortcomings, meant short and shallow dives.

Enter Cousteau, a French naval officer and avid diver. He wasn't satisfied with the status quo and began to experiment. In the late 1930s, Cousteau designed a breathing apparatus that filtered carbon dioxide from exhaled oxygen, then delivered purified air back to the tank. Testing his invention nearly killed him when, during a dive, the recirculated oxygen turned toxic as he passed 45 feet. "My lips began to tremble uncontrollably," Cousteau recalled later. "My eyelids fluttered. My spine was bent backward like a bow. With a violent gesture I tore off the belt weight and lost consciousness." Cousteau floated to the surface, where he was hauled aboard by his boat crew and revived. He suffered pain for weeks.

In 1943, Cousteau and engineer Émile Gagnan built a different device, which they called the Aqua-Lung. This was a demand-valve system that automatically fed divers compressed air with each

On board the *Calypso*, Cousteau was father figure, commander, confessor, principal scientist, chief diver, script doctor and movie director. Once the ship docked, he served as editor and narrator.

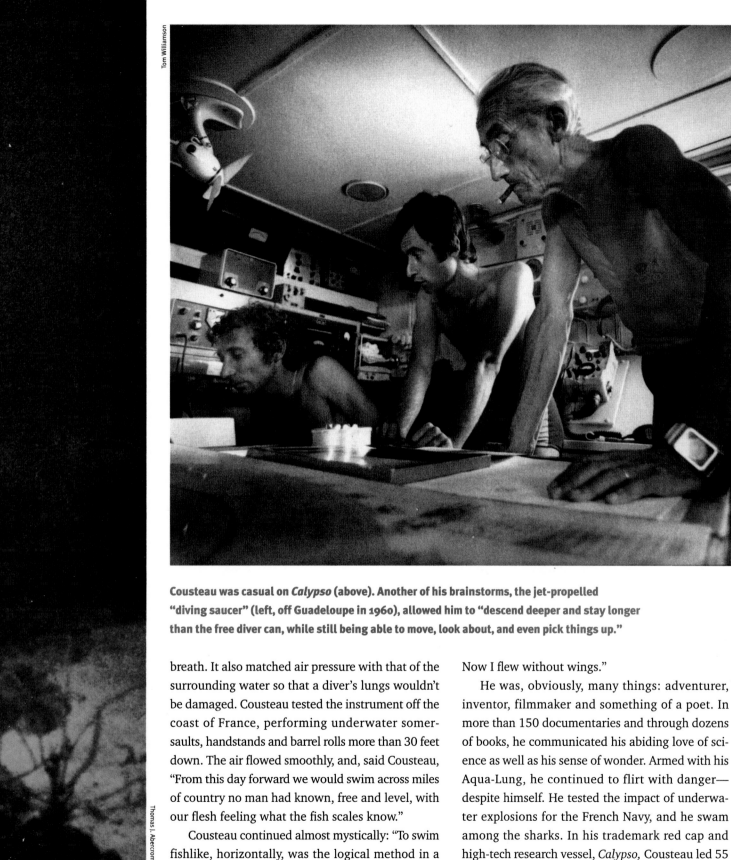

Tom Williamson

Thomas J. Abercrombie/NGS Image Collection

Cousteau was casual on *Calypso* (above). Another of his brainstorms, the jet-propelled "diving saucer" (left, off Guadeloupe in 1960), allowed him to "descend deeper and stay longer than the free diver can, while still being able to move, look about, and even pick things up."

breath. It also matched air pressure with that of the surrounding water so that a diver's lungs wouldn't be damaged. Cousteau tested the instrument off the coast of France, performing underwater somersaults, handstands and barrel rolls more than 30 feet down. The air flowed smoothly, and, said Cousteau, "From this day forward we would swim across miles of country no man had known, free and level, with our flesh feeling what the fish scales know."

Cousteau continued almost mystically: "To swim fishlike, horizontally, was the logical method in a medium eight hundred times denser than air. To halt and hang attached to nothing, no lines or air pipe to the surface, was a dream. At night I often had visions of flying by extending my arms as wings.

Now I flew without wings."

He was, obviously, many things: adventurer, inventor, filmmaker and something of a poet. In more than 150 documentaries and through dozens of books, he communicated his abiding love of science as well as his sense of wonder. Armed with his Aqua-Lung, he continued to flirt with danger—despite himself. He tested the impact of underwater explosions for the French Navy, and he swam among the sharks. In his trademark red cap and high-tech research vessel, *Calypso,* Cousteau led 55 expeditions, in locales from Alaska to Antarctica. He went in search of Atlantis in the Aegean. When he died in 1997, the whole world mourned. We had lost the pied piper of the seven seas.

Divining the Progress of Man

Thor Heyerdahl sought to prove that the ancients got from there to there.

Surrounded by deep, green ocean, Thor Heyerdahl decided to try a simple experiment. He had noticed that the wood of his crude boat, *Kon-Tiki,* was absorbing water, so he cut off a small piece. He dropped it into the waves—and then watched as it sank out of sight. Uh-oh.

It was mid-May 1947, and a few weeks earlier the Norwegian anthropologist had set sail from Callao, Peru, on a balsa raft with five other men, embarking upon what some anthropologists considered a lunatic attempt to prove a bogus migration theory. As the sodden segment of balsa sank

Owen/Black Star (2)

Heyerdahl took the tiller during a storm (opposite). The raft *Kon-Tiki* crossed the Pacific in 101 days, proving that it was possible, whether or not it had been done before.

Kon-Tiki Expedition (2)

into the sea, it might have seemed that the critics were right. One thing, at least, was certain: It was too late to turn back.

When Heyerdahl hatched his idea of navigating a raft across the Pacific in an attempt to confirm that island settlers may have come from the east—that the Polynesians may have hailed from South America—his theorizing was based on slim evidence. Heyerdahl had noted that two cultures separated by thousands of miles of water shared similar plant species, bits of language and a few legends, including one about a god named Tiki. Academics who refused to buy into Heyerdahl's hypothesis pointed out that, for starters, no primitive craft could have survived the journey. The challenge having been issued, Heyerdahl vowed to prove the possibility the only way he could.

Overcoming a lifelong fear of the ocean that had roots in his near drowning as a child, he plunged into preparations, flying to South America to build a copy of the balsa rafts used by South American Indians in ancient times. With the help of local laborers, he and his small crew bound nine 30-to-45-foot balsa logs together, using 300 separate

On a voyage of such duration, endless seas often equated with boredom. The men read, studied, sang songs and landed fish. Certainly some of their fishing was for food, but they invented a shark-rassling game (right), wherein they would grab the fish by the tail and haul it aboard bare-handed.

lengths of hemp rope. Their platform was 750 square feet. They constructed a cabin of bamboo and banana leaves, raised two mangrove masts for a sail and named the rig *Kon-Tiki*.

The pseudomigrants stocked up on native foods—coconuts, sweet potatoes and roots—but supplemented their stores with military rations. In other updates, they devoted a corner of the cabin to radio equipment and toted along cameras, a guitar and dozens of books.

Scientists scoffed and sailors issued dire warnings, but Heyerdahl had his heart and mind set. The crew shoved off on April 28 and over the next 101 days weathered fierce storms and swarming sharks. They feasted on plankton and on flying fish that fairly jumped onto the boat. The craft "lifted up and down like a seabird," as Heyerdahl described it, seawater flowing in through the bottom and draining out again.

The *Kon-Tiki* didn't sink, and after sailing 4,300 miles, Heyerdahl and his crew made landfall on the reef of Raroia in Polynesia, proving that islands in the Pacific could have been reached by balsa raft from South America.

Could have, the critics pointed out, even as Heyerdahl's best-selling 1950 book, *Kon-Tiki,* and a film of the same name (which won an Oscar for Best Documentary) captivated the wider public. Heyerdahl was upset by the continued carping and the assertions that one lucky voyage proved nothing: "I was amazed to find it taken as a sportsman's stunt."

Heyerdahl made steady progress toward securing recognition in the scientific community with thoughtful presentations, three other boat trips and five more books about seaborne civilizations. The medals and honorary degrees started coming as, said Heyerdahl, "I had the pleasure of being accepted step by step."

Today, a half century after the voyage it recounted, *Kon-Tiki* has been translated into 67 languages, and the Kon-Tiki Museum in Heyerdahl's native land draws 300,000 annual visitors. The man himself, at 85, is still at work, performing archaeological research in Spain's Canary Islands and in Sicily, steadfastly trying to connect the dots of ancient cultures. And he has made his peace with the sea. "I often go down and have lunch by the waves," he says. "You know, wherever I have an open sky and nature around me, I am happy."

The Kon-Tiki Museum

His Other Greatest Hits

The idea this time was that the Egyptians were linked with pre-Columbian cultures of the Western Hemisphere. Heyerdahl had two more boats constructed, replicas of ancient Egyptian reed vessels that he dubbed *Ra* and *Ra II*. In 1969, *Ra* failed to make it from Morocco to Barbados, but the next year *Ra II* succeeded. See, said Heyerdahl once more, it could have happened like this. Another book and another film followed.

In 1977, Heyerdahl built a third reed boat and sailed it down the Tigris River to the Persian Gulf, across the Arabian Sea to Pakistan, thence to the Red Sea: 4,000 miles in four months. The purpose of the Tigris expedition was to prove that ancient Sumerians might have made their way to Asia and the Arabian Peninsula. A book and a film ensued.

Heyerdahl also led expeditions to the Maldive Islands and to Easter Island, in quest, as ever, of the "common roots of civilization."

Heyerdahl's 10-ton *Ra* was dragged by 500 Cairo students (right) past the Pyramids to a truck. The 45-foot vessel was then freighted from Alexandria to Morocco, from which it and *Ra II* (above) sailed.

Under the Ice

William Anderson piloted the world's most powerful submarine through a dark, dangerous realm.

Ralph Morse

Peering through his periscope one summer's day in 1958, Commander William R. Anderson didn't like what he saw. "Plainly speaking, it was mean-looking—dirty, ragged, zagged, highly ridged, and hummocked," he would later write in his book, *Nautilus 90 North.*

He was observing dirty, ragged, zagged ice. As skipper of the submarine *Nautilus,* the 37-year-old Navy captain and his crew of 116 were attempting to go where no men had gone before, under the hanging ridges of the polar cap—directly under the North Pole—and out the other side.

A year earlier, Anderson had piloted the 319-foot, 3,180-ton *Nautilus,* the country's first nuclear sub, partway under the Arctic ice. Government officials, pleased with that effort, devised a plan to slink from sea to shining sea—that is, from Point Barrow, Alaska, to the Greenland Sea. Certainly part of their reasoning was to rival the Soviet Union's recent technological success with the Sputnik satellite; yet another part was to determine how feasible the Arctic might be as a shipping route. But just as certainly for Anderson and his men, part of the motivation was the sheer adventure of the voyage.

Before Anderson set off, everything was hush-hush. His preparations for Operation Sunshine left those around him—including his wife and most crewmembers—in the dark. At one point he even assumed an alias, Charles A. Henderson, while taking part in an "ice reconnaissance" mission. Not until *Nautilus* was under way did Anderson reveal its destination to his men, who had thought they were Panama-bound.

The *Nautilus* (above) was a useful weapon, and Anderson (opposite) an intrepid soldier, during the cold war. The historic moment beneath the Pole was recorded in the ship's log (below).

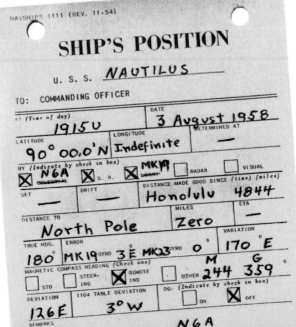

Their first attempt at the Arctic Ocean crossing, in June of '58, failed. They again headed for the ice on July 22. Traveling in a craft that could exceed 20 knots submerged, they spent several perilous days threading through ice that extended eight to 80 feet deep, reading the contours of the ice floes by sonar. They passed beneath the North Pole. Their instruments told them the water was 32.4°F and 13,410 feet deep—almost 2,000 feet deeper than previously thought. The submarine's supplies included cold-weather clothing in case of evacuation, but as the *Nautilus* moved through the depths, its men were well aware that, in the place they were at present, extra layers would do them little good.

As they approached their target on the eastern edge of the ice cap, Anderson said a prayer for world peace.

He later wrote proudly of his boat: "She had blazed a new northwest passage, vastly decreasing the sea-travel time for nuclear submarines from the Pacific to the Atlantic."

Today the first nuclear sub enjoys a serene retirement as the centerpiece of the Historic Ship Nautilus and Submarine Force Museum in Groton, Conn.

Brown Brothers (2)

Into the Trench

Jacques Piccard and **Don Walsh**'s hands-across-the-sea operation plumbed the ocean's depths.

In 1960, seven years after Edmund Hillary and Tenzing Norgay had climbed Mount Everest to the earth's highest point, man had yet to visit its lowest. The Marianas Trench, a deep-sea depression nearly 1,600 miles long and more than 36,000 feet down in the western Pacific Ocean, was alluring—in a creepy sort of way. What was down there, so far beneath the waves off Guam? For anyone to find out, a vessel would be required that could withstand eight tons per square inch of water pressure.

The French-built, U.S. Navy–operated bathyscaph *Trieste* was a 150-ton craft with a six-foot-diameter steel sphere and a 58-foot-long gas tank. Naval Lt. Don Walsh believed in it, and so did Swiss engineer Jacques Piccard, whose father had designed the thing. On January 23, 1960, the two men climbed in and closed the hatch.

After being towed for four days by a U.S. Navy oceangoing tugboat, the *Trieste* (above) sat atop a rough sea, prepared to plunge. Left: Inside, Piccard (at rear) and Walsh checked instruments.

They descended at the rate of four feet per second for five hours, eventually bottoming out at a record 35,800 feet below sea level. "And as we were settling into this final fathom," wrote Piccard in his memoir *Seven Miles Down,* "I saw a wonderful thing." It was a weird fish, he said, flat and with two round eyes on top of its head. "Here, in an instant, was the answer," he wrote. "Could life exist in the greatest depths of the ocean? It could!"

Though scientists would later surmise that Piccard's "fish" was more likely a sea cucumber, no one would argue that Piccard and Walsh's dive hadn't answered another question conclusively. Human beings could survive not only at the planet's highest elevation but also at its greatest depth.

An interesting footnote: Although Japan did send a robot into the Marianas Trench in 1995, no human has ever been back.

Saint Brendan's Odyssey

In trying to prove that an Irish monk might have discovered the New World, **Tim Severin** proceeded with missionary zeal.

Who was Brendan the Navigator? He was an Irish monk born circa 489, died circa 577. He was founder of many monasteries, including the great one at Clonfert, where he lies buried. And, oh, yes, it's possible that dear old Saint Brendan was the very first European to set foot in the New World.

That's right, Saint Brendan may have discovered America way before Leif Eriksson or Christopher Columbus came up with the notion. An ancient narrative history of Brendan's successful quest for a "Promised Land of the Saints" has been translated

Severin named both his expedition and his boat *Brendan*. Nothing like his vessel had sailed the seas in a millennium or more, and though all five crewmembers were seasoned sailors, they struggled to control her.

Ian Yoemans/Severin Archive (2)

Cotton Coulson/Severin Archive

Ancient ways: Severin (above, left) put a stitch in the hull as George Molony looked on. The boat's framework (left and right) featured ash laths bound by leather thongs. Severin found a rare piece of Irish-grown timber tall enough for a mainmast (opposite). When the curragh was complete, Bishop Eammon Casey said a prayer over her: "Bless this boat, O True Christ/Convey her free and safe across the sea . . ./To go to the land of promise is your right/You are like a guide of Brendan's time/Guide our boat now."

into many languages, and while fancy-pants historians will have none of it, arguments are put forward at regular intervals by Hibernophiles. They insist that cave dwellings and Stonehenge-like arrangements throughout northeastern North America reflect a Celtic influence; when a large seaside rock with Irish letters inscribed on it was discovered in Newfoundland three decades ago, Canada's national archivist declared, "There is no doubt that Irish monks reached our shores before the Vikings."

Brendan the Navigator was the most footloose of these monks. Having heard rumors about a land of milk and honey to the west, he set out from Dingle with a crew of more than a dozen men in a 36-

foot, skin-covered boat called a "curragh," or coracle. When he returned, he had many fascinating stories to tell, and oral traditions concerning Brendan were eventually codified in *Navigatio Sancti Brendani Abbatis* ("The Voyage of Saint Brendan the Abbot"). *Navigatio,* written between 800 and 1000, well after Brendan's explorations, was, in its day, a wildly popular read; it remains a tantalizing document. In it, Brendan tells of encountering "mountains in the sea spouting fire," floating crystal pillars, monsters with horns growing from their mouths, and "little furry men." Before dismissing this as all too Tolkien, think upon Iceland's volcanoes, upon icebergs, upon walruses, upon Eskimos.

According to *Navigatio,* Brendan and crew drifted from one island to another for seven years, "following God's stepping stones," until they came to a large landmass where they stayed briefly. Their

return voyage was made by an altogether different route, perhaps via the Azores. The voyage was seen as triumphant, and this view obtained for centuries. It is said that 900 years after Brendan and at least 400 after the publication of *Navigatio,* Christopher Columbus visited Dingle to secure information about Brendan's trip before setting out on his own voyage of discovery. Maybe he did, maybe he did not—but certainly Columbus knew *Navigatio.* A map that he used when sailing from Spain in 1492 featured a large landmass in the middle of the Atlantic labeled "Saint Brendan's Island." In fact, the Spanish crown had already claimed sovereignty over the place—wherever and whatever it was—and many sailors before Columbus had sought to find it. Back then, no one was scoffing at Brendan's claims.

Cut to 1976, and anyone who might know of Brendan's claims would readily and loudly scoff. Anyone but Tim Severin, a British sailor, author, filmmaker and lecturer. Severin was a devotee of *Kon-Tiki*–esque adventures, having already traced Marco Polo's route on a motorcycle (he would go on to re-create journeys of Ulysses, Sinbad and Genghis

Ian Yeomans/Severin Archive

Cotton Coulson/Severin Archive

Arthur Magan (left), wearing Irish woolens more stylish than Brendan might have sported, caught up on modern texts. George Molony, wearing garb far more weather-resistant than Brendan's, pulled the boat ashore in the New World.

Khan). He found Brendan's tale irresistible and sought to replicate it precisely. He located a centuries-old tannery that prepared oxhides in the medieval manner, and with these he fashioned a curragh just like Brendan's. He and his crew set out from Ireland on May 17, seeking to follow the "stepping stones" (thought to be the Hebrides, the Faroes, Iceland, Greenland and Newfoundland, the "Promised Land"). It turns out, indeed, that, were one to traverse the approximately 3,000 miles from Ireland to America, this route would be not only the one with the least open water but also the shortest:

Transatlantic jets use it on the Shannon-to-Boston leg every day.

For more than a year, Severin and company survived wind and terrible weather. At one point the crew repaired a tear in the hull of the boat by hanging over the side as they restitched the leather, their heads sometimes submerged in the icy North Atlantic. Donald S. Johnson wrote of the Brendan Voyage in his 1994 book, *Phantom Islands of the Atlantic:* "On June 26, 1977, they landed in New-foundland. This remarkable achievement ended all controversy over whether such a voyage was possi-ble. Using the prevailing wind and current patterns of northern latitudes, Severin found a 'logical pro-gression' of landfalls, one conceivably the same as Saint Brendan's; the islands he visited and the events he encountered closely paralleled those of the ancient legend." Johnson throws cold water on the message of this replica voyage: "Unfortunately, proof that it *could* be done is not the same as proof that it *was* done." True. But there is another way to look at it. Since we know that Severin made it to North America in a big leather canoe, we are required to ask: Did Brendan?

Titanic Obsession

Bob Ballard had to find the *Titanic*. He simply had to.

Aboard the *Knorr* in September 1985, Ballard (standing, in cap) and his crew monitored the progress of the search vehicle *Argo*. More than two miles below them rested the intact 470-foot forward section of the *Titanic* (left).

Someone should go get Bob." The suggestion was made, but no one moved. All eyes remained focused on a grainy, indistinct image on the computer monitor: the *Titanic*.

Bob—or, rather, Robert Ballard, Ph.D.—was a marine geologist who had spent 19 years at the Woods Hole Oceanographic Institution on Cape Cod, Mass., a dozen years obsessing about the doomed ship *Titanic* and an hour in bed reading Chuck Yeager's autobiography. It was one a.m. on September 1, 1985, and he lay three decks above the control center of the ship *Knorr,* which rolled on the ocean's surface 12,460 watery feet above the rusted hull of the *Titanic.* Ballard, wholly unaware that the *Knorr*'s crew had found the prize, was ready for lights-out.

And then the knock came (the dumbstruck band of French and American researchers having finally sent the ship's cook to go get Bob). Ballard knew immediately what had happened. He pulled on a

jumpsuit and bounded downstairs just in time to see the first identifiable relic of the ship, one of its massive boilers, slide across the screen.

Ballard got no sleep that night, nor during the next four days. The *Knorr*'s 20 days of round-the-clock searching had paid off, and suddenly sleep was the furthest thing from Bob Ballard's mind.

For the world at large, having the *Titanic* found after 73 years rekindled notions of a glamorous, bygone era. For Ballard, the find proved the value of technology for undersea research. In the early 1970s the U.S. research submersible ALVIN, which was based at Woods Hole, had been overhauled to dive as deep as 12,000 feet. Ballard realized immediately that this put the *Titanic* "within our reach." His quest was begun, and even as he worked on other projects, including developing various technologies that would help him find the ship, he kept a wary eye on rival American scientists who had started searching the waters of the North Atlantic.

In the summer of 1985, Ballard teamed with French scientists for a two-phase search. First aboard the French vessel, then on the American ship, they "mowed the lawn," traveling back and forth across 150 square miles of ocean off Newfoundland while

Photomosaic by John Porteus

Woods Hole Oceanographic Institution (6)

More than 100 images were spliced to create a photomosaic of the forward section (top). Artifacts: a doll's head, a bottle, a bathtub, a control instrument, a light fixture, a bench.

towing a video "eyeball" that sent back images to the control room. Two months into the search, the cook was sent for Bob.

Ballard is a self-described "pioneer" who has led more than 100 deep-sea adventures and has published 16 books about his explorations. Nothing got ahold of him like the *Titanic,* however, and since 1985 he has returned to the scene often, exploring the wreck from ALVIN, finding artifacts that lend a poignancy to the tragedy that claimed 1,500 lives:

wine bottles, teacups, a porcelain doll's head, a pair of shoes. Ballard has been critical of other expeditions that have removed items from the *Titanic* and, ever the evangelist for technology, foresees a day when high tech might protect sunken ships from what he considers "graverobbing." Instead of paying to visit the ship or a museum that is displaying its plunder, Ballard says, the buff could repair to his home Internet theater, where he could "go down to the *Titanic* and kick around" for a while.

The Steger Expedition,
Antarctica, 1989

Will Steger / NGS Image Collection

Land

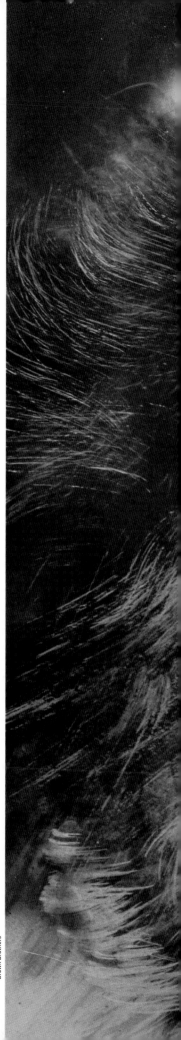

No love was lost between the charismatic Cook, left, and the pugnacious Peary, right. Whatever the merits of their claims, charm, as ever, carried the day in America: One newspaper poll showed 73,238 Cook supporters versus only 2,814 for Peary. Peary was apoplectic; his wife said that the controversy shortened his life.

The Race to the Pole

Robert E. Peary claimed he got there first. But so did **Frederick A. Cook.** Who seized the Arctic Grail?

Ninety-one years after two Americans, Robert Edwin Peary and Frederick Albert Cook, both claimed to have been the first to reach the North Pole, experts are still arguing over which of them—if either—turned the trick. Certainty remains elusive.

Cook's case is weaker, not least because Cook is such a lousy character witness for himself. A physician, he was, to be sure, also an accomplished outdoorsman. He had served as surgeon on Peary's first Arctic expedition in 1891 and had done some serious mountaineering in the years prior to his North Pole assault. But consider the mountaineering as

Peary, in Eskimo garb and with Eskimo dogs, posed on board the *Roosevelt,* his winter quarters for the 1909 attempt.

Exhibit A against the man: In 1906, Cook stated that he had made the first successful ascent of Alaska's Mount McKinley. Later, his summit photographs were revealed as fakes, and Cook's climbing partner recanted his corroboration. Exhibit B could be Cook's conviction for mail fraud, a smear erased—sort of—by a presidential pardon in 1940, the year of Cook's death. So that's Frederick A. Cook.

Peary was no sweetheart either. The U.S. Navy commander was unlikable, arrogant and extraordinarily self-involved. A married man with a son and a daughter, he fathered two Eskimo children during his Arctic adventures. (Though he associated with Eskimos during his entire career, Peary proved to be no friend to the northern people: As detailed in Kenn Harper's *Give Me My Father's Body: The Life of*

The Snow Mother

Though widely scorned by those who believed that the Arctic was no place for a woman, Josephine Peary accompanied her husband on three of his polar expeditions, and during the 1891–92 trip became the first non-native woman to winter in the far north. In 1893 she sailed to the Arctic while pregnant with her first child. Her daughter, Marie Ahnighito, was born in September and spent the first year of her life among the Eskimos, who nicknamed her Ahpoomikaninny: The Snow Baby. Later, Josephine Peary wrote two books detailing Eskimo life, her contributions to her husband's expeditions, and the joys of mothering in one of the coldest places on earth. She was, as her writing made clear, as tough as any Arctic adventurer: "As for cold, hardship, and hunger, that is nonsense. Of course, if I feel so inclined, I can go out and sit on an iceberg until I freeze to it, and let the wind and snow beat upon me, even starve myself; but my tastes do not run in that direction."

The *Roosevelt,* locked in the winter ice at Cape Sheridan, carried 22 expedition members, 49 Eskimos, 246 dogs and, for food, whale, musk ox and walrus meat.

Minik, The New York Eskimo, in 1897 Peary presented six Eskimos as "specimens" to the American Museum of Natural History in New York City. Four of the group died almost immediately of influenza.) Peary once said of Matthew Henson, his African American assistant of 22 years, "Henson must go all the way. I can't make it without him." Throughout the Arctic, Henson cooked, built igloos, tended the dogs and walked every cold and painful step, while his boss was hauled on a sledge by Eskimos. But when evidence indicated that Henson had quite possibly reached the Pole before him (see sidebar on the following pages), Peary never spoke to the man again. So that's Robert E. Peary.

Cook and Peary were right for the task, as the goal they had in sight could be reached only by a

On the *Roosevelt* and on the ice, Henson handled the sledges. Born in 1866, he lived until 1955 and was in all probability the first to stand at the Pole, but he never got the recognition he deserved.

Matthew Henson's Polar Travails

In the race for the North Pole, perhaps the most accomplished of the explorers— certainly the most overlooked—was Matthew Henson, the son of a sharecropper, who had crewed on ships to China, Japan, North Africa and southern Russia before he turned 18. He met Peary at about that age and signed on as "body servant" for an expedition to Nicaragua. As he wrote in his 1912 autobiography, *A Negro Explorer at the North Pole,* Henson would travel with Peary for the next 22 years "in the capacity of assistant: a term that covers a multitude of duties, abilities, and responsibilities."

Henson struggled every inch as far as Peary, while at the same time working to keep expedition members alive and on the move. According to 1908 team member Donald B. MacMillan, Henson, "with years of experience equal to that of Peary himself, was indispensable to Peary and of more real value than the combined services of all four white men . . . He made all the sledges, he made all the camp equipment, he talked the [Eskimo] language like a native."

The Eskimos claimed that nobody drove dogs better than Henson. They said he could fix a broken-down sledge as fast and as well as any of them. During the 1908–09 journey to the Pole, as Peary rode in a sledge, his frostbitten feet all but useless, Henson walked. When the team stopped for the day, Henson built Peary's igloo, took care of the dogs, repaired equipment and hunted hares "with wolfish desperation." Only then did he build shelter for himself.

"After twenty-two long years of service with Peary we are now as strangers," he wrote in the *Boston American* on July 17, 1910. What had happened between the two men? Plenty. Henson went on to say that Peary had intended to make his dash to the Pole without Henson. "I was sorely disappointed," he wrote, "but somehow I had an abiding faith that he was wrong in his calculations." Henson believed they were already at the Pole. After an hour, reported Henson, Peary returned with a "long and serious" face. "He would not speak to me," Henson wrote. "From the moment I declared to Commander Peary that I believed we stood upon the Pole he apparently ceased to be my friend."

Henson tried to mend the rift, attempting to contact Peary but receiving no response. Or hardly any response: After Henson gave a lecture about his adventures, Peary sent a telegram warning him not to use photographs of their expeditions. There was irony to this. Henson claimed that Peary had never returned some 110 images that he—Henson—had paid for, exposed, developed and then lent to Peary.

For the most part ignored by organizations such as the National Geographic Society, which sponsored several of Peary's expeditions, Henson defiantly continued to tell his side of the story. Certainly some did believe him, and in 1937 he was made an honorary member of the Explorers Club.

Henson died in 1955 at age 88 and was buried in New York's Woodlawn Cemetery. In 1988, after a tireless campaign by Harvard professor S. Allen Counter, Henson's remains were transferred to Arlington National Cemetery, where, 68 years earlier, Peary had been interred with great ceremony. On Matthew Henson's headstone are engraved the last words from his memoir: "The lure of the Arctic is tugging at my heart, to me the trail is calling! The Old Trail! The Trail that is always New!"

Royal Geographical Society

At the outer edges of the Arctic ice cap, huge pressure ridges made Peary's progress arduous (above). By the time the team got closer to the Pole (right, five miles from it), the surface was smoother but leads—breaks in the ice—became a threat. Here, the expedition took a sounding, lowering a wire 1,500 fathoms into the ocean but not reaching bottom.

driven man of considerable ego. The North Pole was the single greatest target for adventurers at the turn of the century. In the 1890s the Norwegian Fridtjof Nansen sailed his ship to Spitsbergen but ultimately failed to reach the Pole; the Swede Salomon Andrée tried to reach the Pole by balloon but failed; Peary tried for the Pole on dogsled but failed. The North Pole, floating on a sea 13,410 feet deep, its surface ice perpetually shifting and drifting, cracking and freezing again, was a cruel siren: By the early 20th century it had already claimed the lives of hundreds of adventurers.

Peary, 52, felt certain that his 1908 expedition would be his last. His six previous trips to the Arctic had earned him considerable renown—in 1891–92 he had proved Greenland to be an island

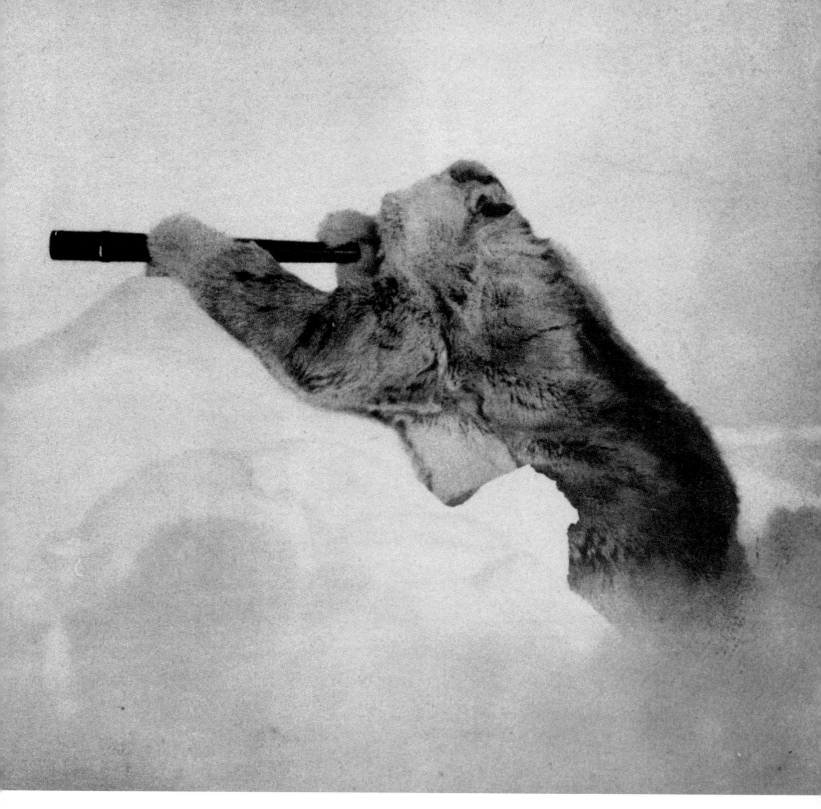

by exploring its northern coast, and his 1905 polar trek had established a farthest-north record—but he would remain unfulfilled if he did not reach 90 degrees north.

He either did or did not do so on April 6, 1909, after an over-the-ice journey of 37 days, accompanied on the last stretch by Henson and four Eskimos. Before Peary could even cable the news, his old colleague Cook blindsided him by announcing from the Shetland Islands that he had stood atop the world a full year earlier. It seemed, initially, that he might have, but the journals he presented as proof were said by experts to have been doctored, and the Eskimo guides that Cook trotted out as witnesses proved as worthy as his McKinley corroborator. The Eskimos finally admitted that Cook had,

Peary scanned the ice cap's horizon in this portrait taken by Henson.

Both of these at-the-top-of-the-world photos—Peary's of his four Eskimos and Henson, center, and Cook's of his two Eskimos with igloo and flag—have been disputed.

in fact, never left sight of land—land that ends hundreds of miles south of the Pole.

In recent years, Peary's claim has also come under a cloud: Did he get there? Were his measurements accurate? The truth may never be known. In 1989 the National Geographic Society, after commissioning the Navigation Foundation to spend more than a year investigating 225 cubic feet of documents, announced that Peary, who had been made a rear admiral before his death in 1920, had very likely come within five miles of the North Pole—and perhaps had stood upon the spot itself. Whatever the truth is, favor does seem to rest much more comfortably with Peary than with Cook. As Peter Freuchen, the noted Danish explorer and writer who knew both men, once put it: "Cook was a liar and a gentleman; Peary was neither."

Steps Toward the North Pole

circa 320 B.C. The Greek Pytheas is said to have discovered a northern land, Thule, which might have been Norway, Iceland or Greenland.

circa 530 A.D. Irish monks are said to have journeyed into the Arctic. One of them, Saint Brendan, might or might not have discovered North America.

900 The Norse explore Greenland.

1576 Sir Martin Frobisher, at Queen Elizabeth's behest, searches for the Northwest Passage from Europe to the Orient.

1607 Henry Hudson, an Englishman, sails to Spitsbergen, islands north of Norway.

1819–45 The Arctic expeditions of Sir John Franklin end with his disappearance after his two ships enter Lancaster Sound in search of the Northwest Passage.

1881–83 The expedition of American Adolphus W. Greely establishes a new farthest-north point.

1888–92 Greenland is explored in separate expeditions led by the Norwegian Fridtjof Nansen and the American Robert E. Peary.

1892 Peary reaches northernmost Greenland.

1893 Peary tries for the Pole.

1893–96 Nansen tries for the Pole.

1897 The Swede Salomon Andrée is killed trying to fly to the Pole in a balloon.

1903–05 Roald Amundsen of Norway, who will be first to reach the South Pole, becomes the first to sail the Northwest Passage.

April 6, 1909 Peary, Matthew Henson and four Eskimos reach the Pole—maybe.

Nansen (above) was one of the great Arctic adventurers, while Andrée (below) was the greatest of northern balloonists.

Triumph and Tragedy

Culver Pictures

Roald Amundsen and **Robert Falcon Scott** dashed to the South Pole. One of them returned glorious. One didn't return.

Starvation near at hand, an exhausted Ernest Shackleton stumbled, in 1907, to a spot a mere 97 miles from the South Pole, then turned back. The Norwegian explorer Roald Amundsen had kept close watch. Shackleton, he said, "had managed to lift the veil that rested over Antarctica . . . But a little patch remained."

The race was on.

In the first decade of the century, Amundsen was focusing on both the North and South Poles, neither of which had been reached by man, and after pio-

Amundsen (above) had one eye on Peary's North Pole trek and the other on Scott's South Pole effort. In 1911, Scott's team (right) was established in Antarctica.

Popperfoto

neering the Northwest Passage from 1903 to 1906, it was evident that he had a good chance of being the first man to stand on the North Pole. But which way to turn? One of his principal rivals in questing after the Antarctic Grail was the Englishman Robert Falcon Scott, who had, before Shackleton, come close to the South Pole during a 1901–04 expedition—Shackleton had been a member of Scott's crew—and was preparing for another assault. By 1909, Scott, 41, was outfitted and ready to go. So

was Amundsen, but he was intending to take his ship, crew and dogs north. Then the news broke: Robert Peary had reached the North Pole. "This was a blow indeed!" Amundsen wrote in his 1927 autobiography. "If I was going to maintain my prestige as an explorer I must quickly achieve a sensational success of some sort."

Amundsen, 37, had trained for his Arctic exploration with gusto, had mortgaged his house and had borrowed from fellow explorer Fridtjof Nansen the famous ship *Fram*. He had to do something with all this preparation. He set sail, and only when he was a month under way did he reveal to his crew and backers that the goal was now the South Pole. Then he wired Scott: BEG LEAVE TO INFORM YOU FRAM PROCEEDING ANTARCTIC AMUNDSEN.

Scott was shocked and dismayed. Amundsen, a professional explorer who had already wintered 11 times in polar regions, was an expert skier and handler of Greenland sled dogs. Scott, a captain in the Royal Navy, was a man of considerable insecurities, and his diaries reveal that he was aware of this. "How can I bear it?" he once wrote in his journal.

The *Fram* (left) delivered Amundsen and his men to Antarctica, while Scott's ship (opposite) was the *Terra Nova*. The photographer Herbert G. Ponting was delighted when he found, in an iceberg near Scott's first camp, a grotto that made a perfect frame for the ship. Amundsen (top left) was comfortable on skis and used them to great advantage during his dash. Scott (above) disdained his skis.

AKG Photo

H. Ponting/Royal Geographical Society (2)

Brown Brothers

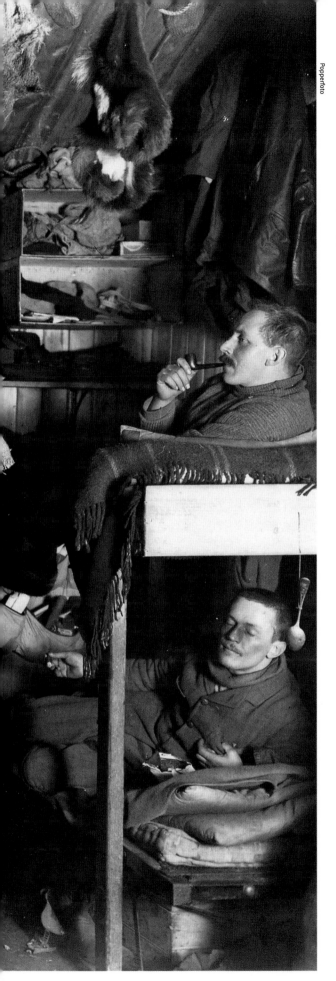

"I write of the future; of the hopes of being more worthy; but shall I ever be?" Facing the imposing Amundsen's challenge, Scott wondered if he could possibly prevail.

Upon reaching land, Scott set up camp at Cape Evans on the mainland of Ross Island, where he suffered some punishing winds. Amundsen chose to establish quarters on a glacier in the Bay of Whales, where he was relatively protected from wind. Another advantage: The Norwegian's camp was 60 miles south of Ross Island—10 percent closer to the Pole.

Scott, for reasons not wholly known, took four compatriots with him on his final dash instead of the originally planned three, further stressing an already inadequate food and fuel supply. Amundsen calculated rations to the last meal and kept his men well fed, even increasing their portions on particularly tough days. He had stashed three times as much fuel as Scott.

Scott had packed skis, but he and his men were

Anatomy of Starvation

For more than 100 days, Scott's party existed on a daily per-man ration of 16 oz. of biscuits, 0.57 oz. of cocoa, 12 oz. of pemmican—a meat jerky of sorts—2 oz. of butter, 3 oz. of sugar and 0.7 oz. of tea. The men ingested an average of 4,500 calories a day while burning more than 6,000. Their diet was utterly lacking in vitamin C, and eventually scurvy set in, preventing fresh wounds from healing, meanwhile dissolving scars and causing old wounds to reopen.

inexpert and soon after strapping them on decided they were cumbersome and dangerous for travel over ragged fields of crevasse and ice ridge. Amundsen and his men had grown up on skis, and used them regularly during their eight-week trip across the ice cap.

Perhaps Scott's biggest mistake was his decision, against the expert advice of the esteemed Nansen, to rely on ponies to haul supplies—and then, in this desperate, lifeless place, to care about his ponies' survival. The animals proved vulnerable to the cold, and each night Scott's men used dwindling energy in building snow walls to shelter the beasts. Their long, hoofed legs sank deep into the snow, and the ponies quickly deteriorated. Scott was beyond saddened, he was horrified, and he shunned his teammates' advice to put the animals out of their misery, then store the horsemeat along the route as food for both men and dogs. One by one the ponies died, and Scott and his men were left to drag the supply sledges on their own, sometimes advancing only a few miles in a day.

Amundsen's dogs, meanwhile, could cover 20 miles in a five-hour day, and then, after feasting on seal or even a fellow canine's flesh, would dig themselves in for the night. Amundsen had dogs killed in sequence, their meat stashed at depots where it would be eaten on the return.

Scott's team traveled with ponies (above), which turned out to be a costly mistake. Amundsen (opposite) relied on dogs and skis, and this proved a highly efficient way to go.

Steps Toward the South Pole

1773–75 Britain's Capt. James Cook enters the Antarctic at 71 degrees 10 minutes south, the first man to cross the Antarctic Circle. He doesn't prove that the Antarctic continent exists, and says no one will: "I can be bold enough to say that no man will ever venture further than I have done and that the lands which may be the South will never be explored."
1819–21 Capt. Fabian von Bellingshausen makes the first landfall inside the Circle, discovering Peter I and Alexander I islands for Russia, while the American Nathaniel Palmer discovers Palmer Peninsula.
1823 James Weddell, an Englishman searching for new sealing grounds, discovers the Weddell Sea.
1840 While the Englishman James Clark Ross discovers the Great Ice Barrier and records magnetic observations that will aid explorers who come after him, the American Charles Wilkes explores 1,500 miles of the Antarctic coast.
1895 Norwegian whaler Leonard Kirstensen and his men are the first to step on the continent of Antarctica.
1897 Adrien de Gerlache of Belgium winters below the Antarctic Circle; the Norwegian Roald Amundsen is in his party.
1901–04 The Englishman Robert Falcon Scott discovers Edward VII's Peninsula.
1907–09 Ernest Shackleton of Great Britain leads an expedition to within 97 miles of the South Pole.
1908 Douglas Mawson of Australia reaches the South Magnetic Pole.
1908–09 Shackleton explores the continent on Manchurian ponies.
1911 Amundsen's expedition reaches the South Pole on December 14 via dogsled.
1912 Scott's party reaches the Pole, but all five die on the return trip.

Amundsen, four teammates, four sledges and 52 dogs reached the Pole on December 14, 1911. They had covered 714 miles in 57 days. They would complete the entire round-trip in 100 days. In all this time, their greatest discomfort would be one man's toothache. By way of contrast: While Scott and his men were struggling toward starvation, Amundsen's charges were ski-racing like kids down the Axel Heiberg glacier.

On January 17, 1912, Scott gained the Pole, having already lost the race. He found the Norwegian flag and Amundsen's tent—and the prospect of an 800-mile return trip burdened by failure. The expedition had been on the ice 78 days and would trudge another nine weeks, frostbitten and often delirious. After becoming trapped in a furious blizzard, they would starve to death—11 miles short of their last depot, 177 miles from their winter quarters.

Amundsen won the South Pole, but Scott, with his struggle recounted posthumously in moving, literate journals, won the world's heart. This, from "The Last March":

"Every day we have been ready to start for our depot eleven miles away, but outside the door of the tent it remains a scene of whirling drift. I do not think we can hope for any better things now. We shall stick it out to the end but we are getting weaker of course and the end cannot be far.

"It seems a pity but I do not think I can write more—

R. Scott

"Last Entry—For God's sake look after our people."

Upon gaining the Pole, Amundsen took a sighting (above), then treated his men to seal meat. Once Scott found Amundsen's tent 1.5 miles from 90 degrees south (opposite, bottom), he knew he had lost the race. The expressions of his team at the Pole (opposite, top) were grim.

we shall stick it out to the end but we are getting weaker of course and the end cannot be far.
It seems a pity but I do not think I can write more —
R Scott
Last entry.
For Gods sake look after our people

Everest

Simply by being there, a Himalayan peak posed the ultimate challenge.

The 1924 British team included, from left (rear), Sandy Irvine, George Mallory, Edward Norton, Noel Odell, (London) *Times* photo runner John Macdonald, and (front) E.O. Shebbeare, Geoffrey Bruce, Howard Somervell and Bentley Beetham. Beetham photographed the route to the top from East Rongbuk Glacier (above).

There had been 32 years of expeditions, and at least 13 lives lost, by the time Edmund Hillary and Tenzing Norgay set off for the world's highest peak in 1953. "There was much talk about 'unjustifiable risk,'" recalled Hillary in his autobiography. "But I think we all realized that these were attitudes from the past, that nobody was going to get up Everest without a few risks."

The attitude of the distant past held that Everest was a mystical, spiritual realm—Chomolungma to the Tibetans: Mother Goddess of the Earth. It was seen by many foreigners as a forbidding, impossible place. But by the late 1800s, climbing was being done throughout the Himalayas, and there were men, most of them British, who were wondering how to conquer Everest.

They didn't know anything about what that might entail. Not only didn't they know how, or if, they could overcome Everest's avalanches, collapsing ice, crevasses, bitter cold and relentless wind, they were by no means certain that a man could survive—could breathe, could remain intact—at

29,028 feet above sea level. What would happen to the body? Might one conquer the mountain only to have the mountain take one's life as payment?

There were some, certainly, who would have none of such hoodoo. "To my mind at least, as far as human endurance is concerned, it would be no more surprising to me to hear that a man had succeeded in walking up Mt. Everest than to know that a man can succeed in standing an arctic climate while on a sledging expedition," Clinton Thomas Dent wrote way back in 1885. "I do not for a moment say that it would be wise to ascend Mt. Everest, but I believe most firmly that it is humanly possible to do so; and, further, I feel sure that even in our own time, perhaps, the truth of these views will receive material corroboration."

Dent was right about the plausibility but off on the timing—although this wasn't exclusively on account of the rock pile's indomitability. There were, in Dent's day and for a good while thereafter, political as well as physical and psychological barriers to conquering Everest. Nepal and Tibet were, in the early decades of the last century, "closed" countries; therefore, access to most of the world's highest peaks was problematic. Lord Curzon, viceroy of India, wrote to Douglas Freshfield of the Royal Geographical Society in 1899 that he, Curzon, would

appeal to Nepal for permission to scale Everest. Military action in Tibet precluded any such endeavor for several years, and in 1905, Curzon wrote to Freshfield again: "It has always seemed to me a reproach that with the second highest mountain in the world for the most part in British territory [K2 in Kashmir] and with the highest in a neighbouring and friendly state, we, the mountaineers and pioneers par excellence of the universe, make no sustained and scientific attempt to climb to the top of either of them." He detailed his plans for an expedition escorted by Swiss guides and "coolies" that might, in the next summer or two, establish successively higher camps "until one day the advance camp would be placed on a spot from which a dash could be made for the summit . . . Ought we not to be able to do this?"

Political problems—complicated ones involving India, Nepal, Tibet and Russia, which some British diplomats did not want to provoke with any maneuvering in the mountains—said the answer was no. A scheduled assault in 1907 was scotched at the last minute by bureaucrats, and for myriad reasons no expedition was mounted until 1921. A dozen other attempts—most of them British, some of them solo, some of them covert—failed during the next three decades.

N.E. Odell

Near Things and Nut Cases

Not every expedition on Everest from 1921 to 1953 had the summit in sight—there were several "reconnaissances" on the mountain—but those listed here all did. Some obviously stood a better chance than others.

1921 British Expedition: Nine team members, including Mallory, run out of gas.

1922 British Expedition: Seven Sherpas are killed by an avalanche below North Col.

1924 British Expedition: Mallory and Irvine disappear into thin air.

1933 British Expedition: The team fails to surpass the previous high point.

1934 Wilson's Solo: Crossing into Tibet in disguise, former British Army Capt. Maurice Wilson dies at 20,997 feet.

1936 British Expedition: The team finds the

North Col's slopes "not impossible" but doesn't conquer them.

1938 British Expedition: A small team reaches 27,296 feet in the final attempt before the onset of the Second World War.

1947 Denman's Solo: Disguised as a Tibetan and climbing with two Sherpas, Earl Denman, a Canadian, nearly reaches the North Col.

1951 Larsen's Solo: Crossing into Nepal surreptitiously, K.B. Larsen of Denmark enlists a dozen Sherpas who then refuse to climb up the North Col, forcing Larsen to give up.

1952 Swiss Expeditions: Pre- and postmonsoon attempts, each with Sherpa Tenzing Norgay as a member, barely fail.

1952 Soviet Expedition: Reportedly, six die as a team approaching from Tibet seeks the summit.

1953 British Expedition: A strong unit makes the first ascent.

Or did they?

In Everest lore and legend, no name is writ larger than that of George Herbert Leigh Mallory—not Hillary's, not Tenzing's, not Jon Krakauer's. A British schoolteacher, Mallory was a brave and dogged climber. When sickness forced Harold Raeburn to step down as climbing leader of the First Everest Reconnaissance Expedition, Mallory took the role. He and Guy Henry Bullock found the approach over the East Rongbuk Glacier to the North Col during that autumn of 1921, but the nine-man team spent far too many weeks at altitude and eventually, sapped of strength, was forced to descend, defeated. In 1922, Mallory was on the second British try

as well; two of his companions got within 1,732 feet of the top, but that was it.

Mallory returned with the Third Everest Expedition in 1924. On June 4, group leader Lt. Col. Edward Felix Norton established a new high by reaching an altitude of 28,126 feet. The big question brought back by the Third Expedition was: Did Mallory perhaps eclipse Norton's achievement on June 8?

On that day, along with his climbing partner, Andrew Comyn "Sandy" Irvine, a 22-year-old engineering student, Mallory set off for a summit that was only 2,000 feet distant. At 12:50 p.m., teammate Noel Odell saw the two men as "black spots"

below the summit, moving forward with alacrity. Mallory and Irvine disappeared into the clouds, "going strong for the top." They were never seen alive again. An ice ax belonging to one of the men was found by the Fourth British Expedition, which nine years later reached the same height as Norton. The discovery of the ax did nothing to solve a mountaineering mystery that, at intervals, has devolved into an unpleasant controversy: Did Mallory and Irvine reach the top? Naysayers insist that they wouldn't have had time that day to summit. The position of Mallory's supporters was poetically expressed early on by Tom Longstaff, a friend of both Mallory and Irvine, who had climbed with the British team in 1922. "It was my good luck to know both of them: such splendid fellows.

"Mallory wrote in the last letter I got from him, 'we are going to sail to the top this time and God with us—or stamp to the top with our teeth in the wind.' I would not quote an idle boast, but this wasn't—they got there alright. Somehow they were 4 hours late, but at 12:50 they were less than 800 ft below and only a quarter of a mile away from the summit: Odell reports them moving quickly: therefore the oxygen was working well; nothing could have stopped these two with the goal well in their grasp at long last." Or, as another associate, Winthrop Young, put it in a letter to *The Times* of London: "the peak was first climbed, because Mallory was Mallory."

Such strong boosterism was not, of course, proof—and it was long thought that proof would

In 1999, Mallory's body was found at 26,800 feet. In his pockets were (top) glacier glasses, a broken altimeter and a pocketknife that was closed when discovered. Also brought back from the site were fragments of Mallory's clothing (above).

never be forthcoming. Then, on May 1, 1999, the Mallory and Irvine Research Expedition, an operation led by American mountain guide Eric Simonson, found Mallory's frozen corpse on a wind-scoured ledge at nearly 27,000 feet—several hundred feet below where the ice ax, identified as Irvine's, was found in 1933. Mallory, still in fur-lined leather helmet and hobnailed boots, a frayed rope around his waist, lay facing upslope, his body frozen into the earth. One leg was broken, an elbow injured. In his forehead was a puncture that exposed part of his brain. On May 17, expedition members found a 1924 oxygen bottle 65 feet above the site of the ax; evidence seemed to be pushing Mallory and Irvine ever farther up the hill. The 1999 expedition, spurred by its finds, continued to search— but found nothing conclusive. They were particularly disappointed not to find the camera, which might contain pictures of the men on the summit.

To most experts, it is clear from the evidence that Mallory fell to his death. Some analysts of the scene maintain that we now know the two climbers were descending when Mallory, in the lead, fell. Irvine likely tried to arrest the fall, but then the rope that connected them snapped, and Mallory plummeted to his death. Though Irvine's body has never been recovered, it is surmised that he, alone and exhausted, with little or no oxygen remaining, perished during the bitter night.

It's all surmise still. From where were they descending? The summit? The Second Step, a wall of rotten rock that took ace rock climber Conrad Anker an hour to climb during the Mallory and Irvine Research Expedition? If the "black spots" Odell saw on the ridge at 12:50 p.m. were Mallory and Irvine, they probably could not have reached the summit until seven p.m., quite possibly as late as three o'clock the next morning. Wouldn't they have turned back much earlier, knowing that an overnight in the Everest cold would almost surely kill them?

"The mystery of Mallory and Irvine therefore lives on," wrote Peter Firstbrook, an expedition member, in *The Search for Mallory & Irvine.* "In death, as in life, they remain together on the mountain; they are in every sense, *the* men of Everest."

They were not, of course, the last men of Everest. Prominent among those who would follow were New Zealander Edmund Hillary and a Nepali named

IN·MEMORY
·OF·THREE·
·EVEREST·
EXPEDITIONS

1921
KELLAS

1922
LHAKPA
NARBU
PASANG

PEMA
SANGE
TEMBA

1924
MALLORY
IRVINE

Tenzing Norgay, born to Sherpas in 1914. Norgay was by age 19 already a porter and mountaineer; before joining the British expedition of 1953, he had climbed on five Everest assaults, Swiss and British, in 1935, '38, '47 and two in '52. By the time he signed on with the Brits again in '53, he probably had spent more time on the mountain than any other man. He had also come the closest to its summit, in 1952, when he and a Swiss teammate were forced back barely 1,000 feet from the top. "The pull of Everest was stronger for me," Norgay, who died in 1986, once said, "than any force on earth."

As for Edmund Hillary . . . Let's hear it from the man himself. In the following pages, the world's greatest living adventurer tells his own story in his own words.

Before leaving for home, the 1924 expedition built a cairn at base camp that commemorated those who had died in British attempts since 1921. The rocks have long since been taken by souvenir hunters.

A Visit with the World's Greatest Living Adventurer

In 1953, Mount Everest was conquered, and the names of an Auckland bee farmer, Edmund Hillary, and his Sherpa climbing partner, Tenzing Norgay, joined those of Peary, Amundsen and Lindbergh atop the hill of 20th century adventuring giants. Of those five, only Hillary is alive; Tenzing died in India in 1986. Sir Edmund, 81, still lives in Auckland, where he resides with his second wife, the former June Mulgrew.

Since summiting on Everest, Sir Edmund has registered numerous other adventuring triumphs in Asia and Antarctica; has served as a diplomat for the New Zealand government; has become a revered figure in Nepal by leading efforts to build dozens of schools and hospitals; has experienced devastating loss when his first wife, Louise Mary Rose, and one of their two daughters died in a plane crash in the Himalayas in 1975; has shared his son Peter's elation when, on his fourth attempt, Peter conquered Everest in 1990; and has—with a certain degree of reluctance—seen his own persona evolve into that of a living legend.

If I needed confirmation of Sir Edmund's exalted status not only in the adventuring pantheon but in that of the world itself, it came when my taxi dropped me off in the driveway of the great man's comfortable home on Remuera Road. I reached into my pocket and peeled off a couple of bills to pay the fare. They were New Zealand five-dollar notes, and they bore the mountaineer's picture. I was going to interview New Zealand's Abe Lincoln.

Sir Edmund—his friends call him Ed—met me at the door; his wife was out. He is a large, strong man still, larger even than the sinewy climber who scaled the heights. His torso is thick. He has bushy eyebrows and a bushy head of salt-and-pepper hair, as untamed today as it was in all those pictures of him in the wilderness. He looms large, as befits a legend, but he is a gentle man.

He invites me in and then, in his sun-soaked living room, gives me all the time I require. He is smart, direct, self-effacing—yet properly proud—just as he was on the occasion of his historic ascent.

—Robert Sullivan

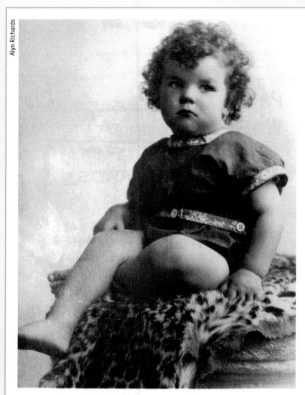

Born in Auckland on July 20, 1919, young Ed was smaller than most classmates at Tuakau Primary School, and there was no telling early on that he was destined for the kind of glory he would gain on Everest alongside Norgay (right).

Robert Sullivan: Tell us about your youth.

Sir Edmund Hillary:

I was born here in Auckland, but the first 15 years of my life we lived 40 miles south in a small village called Tuakau, and I went to primary school there. My mother was a schoolteacher and very keen that I go to a city school, so although it was fairly impoverished times, I traveled every day to the Auckland Grammar School. I found the city rather trying. I was definitely very much a country boy.

I was a really weedy 11-year-old. I grew five inches one year and six inches the next year, and at the end I was large in size.

My relationship with the mountains actually started when I was 16. Every year a group used to be taken from Auckland Grammar down to the Tangariro National Park for a skiing holiday. I think we must have had a good honey season that year, because I was able to persuade my father to let me go on this particular trip. We went down to Ruapehu, and I can remember it just as clearly as when it happened. Our train from Auckland arrived at the National Park station and there was snow everywhere, there was snow on the railroad line, and there was snow on the trees. It was a bright moonlit night, and the moonlight was a brilliant, marvelous sight to me, and it was really

the most exciting thing that ever happened to me up to that time—us rushing around skiing. I found I was reasonably energetic and I could rush around and make snowballs, whatever. That was really the start of my enthusiasm for snow and ice and mountains in general. For a few years I skied whenever I could.

Downhill skiing?

Downhill. I enjoyed it immensely, although I never became a great skier. When I was 50 years old, I actually decided to draw up a list of half a dozen things that I really hadn't done very well, and I was going to make efforts to improve. One of them was skiing, and I did become a very much better skier.

What were some of the other things?

Mostly adventurous activities I wanted to do in the Himalayas, in Antarctica. I was successful, actually, on all the projects. Even when you're 50 you can make the effort to improve your standards.

After that trip when you were young, did you know you were going to go in that direction, and become an accomplished outdoorsman?

No, I didn't visualize myself becoming a renowned mountaineer. It happened gradually. I did a lot of hiking in the hills outside Auckland, and then I started modest mountaineering, and then I was able to do harder climbs, and finally I became a reasonably accomplished mountaineer in the New Zealand Alps and I did a number of treks. I'm inclined to think that happens to a lot of people. Very few suddenly decide they're going to be a world champion at something.

Concerning the allure of hiking and mountaineering: Some people love it because of the solitude, and choose to do it alone. Some like the teamwork. Some do it because of the thrill. What was it for you?

I enjoyed climbing with other people, good friends, but I did quite a lot of solo climbing, too. If I wished to do something, even if I couldn't find anyone who wanted to make the effort with me, I would go out solo climbing. I did find solo climbing very challenging, and a little frightening. You knew that you were completely on your own, and you had to overcome all the problems and possible dangers. Quite demanding, and quite an interesting experience.

Did you enjoy the tingle of fear?

I think I found fear a very stimulating factor. I'm sure the feeling of fear, as long as you can take advantage of it and not be rendered useless by it, can make you extend yourself beyond what you would regard as your capacity. If you're afraid, the blood seems to flow freely through the veins and you really do feel a sense of stimulation. If you can summon up your determination and motivation to overcome the fear, you seem to have more energy to tackle the problem and overcome it.

Did you find that you were more or less fearful by nature than your comrades?

I used to think that I was more fearful than my companions, but in later years, I discovered that they, like myself, concealed very much their fears. I think most people, when they're in a dangerous situation, or potentially dangerous situation, have that sense of fear. I was almost ashamed at times that I was fearful while my companions seemed to be drumming along. I found out later, in talking to them, that they were just as scared as I was.

Do you remember your first brush with fear?

The first peak I climbed in [New Zealand's] southern mountains was a very old route, but we had to climb up a long, steep snow-slope. I was aware that if I slipped on the slope I could possibly injure myself. I was aware that I had to be careful and there was danger. It was really a very small possibility of danger compared to my later situations, but at that time I was keenly aware of it. Getting up to the top of this little mountain and down again gave me probably as much pleasure as climbing a really difficult mountain did later on.

You became a serious climber on New Zealand's South Island.

Yes, but although I did a lot of climbing in New Zealand and a lot of backpacking and walking around the hills, I was a relatively late starter as a "serious" mountaineer. When I first went to the Himalayas in 1951, I was 31 years old. I really was at my prime, though some would think I was getting on. Himalayan climbers tend to mature fairly late. I think most of the successful Himalayan climbers have ranged from 28 to just over 40. When you're younger you're probably

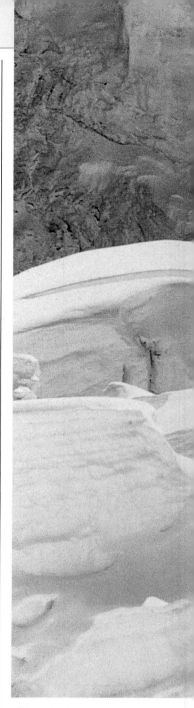

Hillary had two years' experience climbing in the Austrian Alps and two years' trekking in the Himalayas by the time the British expedition of '53 started up Everest (above).

faster, but when you're older you have incredible endurance, and you also have a good deal more experience—you've had more experience being uncomfortable and miserable, whereas the younger person who is all *go, go,* really hasn't been all that miserable in his life. When you're climbing at high altitudes, life can be a pretty miserable business, and I think the older person is able to put up with this more easily than younger people.

So you had gained experience in the Southern Alps, you were part of a group of talented New Zealand climbers that included your friend George Lowe, you had joined these British expeditioners and, at 31, off you went to the Himalayas?

I was involved in two [Himalayan] expeditions in 1951, and then another one in 1952, before doing the top of Everest. I remember in 1951, we got to Australia to head for the Himalayas and we were interviewed by a large number of press people in Sydney. When we told them we weren't going to climb Mount Everest, they completely lost interest in us. One chap from one of the main Sydney papers, when I told him we weren't going to Everest, his face dropped. He said to me, "Have you ever been close to death?" And I said, "Well, I

and one pair of thin socks, which really was completely inadequate for climbing at high altitude in the Himalayas. Even though I had pretty good resistance to cold in my feet, that first trip I definitely had cold feet.

But we still made a lot of new summits, and we did extremely well. We weren't using oxygen that trip. The highest mountain we climbed was just over 22,000 feet.

How many mountains were there?

This was one of the great pleasures, really: We were in an area where almost nobody had done any climbing, and we made six first ascents of mountains over 20,000 feet. That sort of experience is very difficult to come by these days. There are still lots of mountains around, but all the big ones have been done. Reinhold Messner was the first to reach the summit of all the 8,000-meter peaks [a feat the Italian mountaineer completed in 1986].

You were known as an aggressive climber in your Himalayan years.

I was quite competitive, and I tended to compete with members of my own expedition. I don't think I was unpleasantly aggressive, but I think I rather enjoyed grinding my companions into the ground on a big hill.

I remember when [Everest expedition leader] John Hunt and I were walking in from Kathmandu to Everest, we crossed over a river and had to climb up a very long, steep hill. We were going to camp at the top of the hill. I always used to enjoy going fast up these hills, and at one stage I caught up to John, who was about a decade older than I was. I passed him. John was very, very competitive, and even though he was older than me, he really put on the pace to try and pass me again. Well, there was simply no way I would permit anybody to pass me, and I put on the speed and left John behind. I always remember looking behind at John, who was absolutely desperate to try and defeat me on this hill, and I really couldn't understand it. Here was the leader of the expedition, the big wheel, why should he be so desperately keen to beat someone who was a great deal younger than he was?

I was physically strong back then, and I acclimatized well, and I had quite a competitive

don't know. I've been scared a few times." He asked, "Has anybody ever died in the course of your trips?" And I said no. And he said to me, "Gosh, nothing exciting?"

He was a real tough Sydney reporter. I quite liked him, but he was very disappointed in us.

When you first saw the Himalayas, were you awestruck?

No. When we first saw the Himalayan peaks, I was very impressed—they looked pretty good— but they didn't look all that different from what I'd been climbing in the Southern Alps.

Did you find yourselves up to the task?

Yes, I think so. Our first trip was very much a shoestring operation—we were pretty impoverished and most of our equipment was inadequate. For instance, I had a pair of boots which were very primitive and had rubber soles on them, and they were much too small for me, so I could only wear about one pair of thick socks

Hillary hadn't met expedition leader John Hunt (above) until arriving in Kathmandu. "I was immediately impressed. He greeted me with great warmth, told me he was expecting much of me."

Jim Burke

Hillary knew Norgay (left) by reputation and was eager to meet him. "I certainly wasn't disappointed. Tenzing really looked the part— larger than most Sherpas, very strong and active."

spirit. Technically, I was a good snow-and-ice technician, as far as the standards in those days went. I was a good step-cutter and could climb incredible snow and ice pretty effectively. Things have changed so much that the technical ability of people like Messner is greatly superior to anything that we had. But I wouldn't say the modern mountaineer is any stronger, and he certainly is not more strongly motivated.

The Everest expedition was, by the standards of the day, a very professional one.

I think it was well organized, but I wouldn't have said we were very heavily funded. We were a relatively small expedition.

How many were you?

There were really only 11 foreign climbing members, and then Tenzing, who became a climbing member. So there were really only 12 of us who were climbing Everest, and there were three other people—there was the film cameraman, the doctor and James Morris, the press bloke. So there were only 14 or 15 of us.

After us came those really huge expeditions: the Japanese and Italian expeditions, with 50 or 60 people on them and vast numbers of Sherpas. Ours was nothing compared to what came afterwards.

And you were in a competition?

It was definitely a race, and all eyes were on it. The Swiss had two attempts scheduled [in spring and autumn of '52], and we were in the mountains climbing around and listening for news. We were really quite concerned as to whether or not the Swiss would be successful. We didn't wish them any harm at all, we were quite respectful of them really. But we just hoped that they wouldn't be successful getting to the top.

The Swiss put in a particularly good effort, getting to 28,000 feet. That's when Tenzing really came into his own. He teamed up with

Members of the British expedition and their team of Sherpas (above) would eventually pitch nine high-altitude camps during April and May.

[Raymond] Lambert, and Lambert and Tenzing were a pretty formidable combination.

Postmonsoon, the Swiss had bad weather and didn't get as high.

How did you and Tenzing become a team in '53?

The person I really enjoyed climbing with most was George Lowe, and I still believe that if George and I had been in the final summit push, we would have made it because we were a very strong combination. But John decided George and I were both useful as snow-and-ice climbers, and he split us up and used us with different groups. So I realized I simply wasn't going to be able to climb with George. I looked around and decided that the best and fastest mover around the place, apart from myself, was Tenzing.

I remember once, at lower altitudes, going up to this pass. On the walk up, Tenzing and I really raced up to the pass. I beat him to it. But he was obviously very fit, very strong and I was impressed. Tenzing was very competitive too, he wanted to be up front. That was a good sign. And he was a good, sound mountaineer. He had been on quite a few Everest expeditions. He really started as just an ordinary porter on the north side of Everest, and then, since he was obviously strong and accomplished, he became a very useful technical climber as well.

Was he a congenial mate?

Yes, very, very. It wasn't easy to communicate with him in those days. Although he spoke a certain amount of English, we couldn't discuss the philosophy of life, that kind of thing. But mountaineering decisions and so on, he was able to deal with those.

Do you remember the climb vividly?

I remember it pretty vividly. I remember we almost broke down on the Lhotse Face. George and I and the Sherpas were on the Lhotse Face, and we simply weren't making any progress for a week or so. I persuaded John to let Tenzing and me go up and start things moving again—otherwise we simply weren't going to get anywhere—and finally he agreed. We did that and we shot up. It was Tenzing, me and Wilf Noyce. We climbed to 24,000 feet, and we sort of got things rolling again.

A bit later, when the big lift to the South Col was imminent, the party was making very slow

Norgay (left) and Hillary checked oxygen at 22,000 feet before carrying supplies up to the assault camp at 27,900 feet.

progress, and once again I persuaded John that Tenzing and I should go up quickly and then more or less lead them up to the South Col. John somewhat reluctantly agreed. John wanted me and Tenzing not to wear ourselves out before the final push. But I was perfectly O.K.

We had the meeting to talk about the summit strategy and who would make the final push. It really wasn't tense for me. I would have been very surprised if Tenzing and I had not been given the

Alfred Gregory/Royal Geographical Society

As Hillary (left) and Norgay climbed, tethered, toward the Southeast Ridge, the Lhotse Face was a dramatic backdrop. Hillary fixed a tent near 26,000 feet (below). Within days, he photographed Norgay on the summit (opposite).

job of making the final assault.

We established our last camp at just under 28,000 feet. I can remember there were some very fierce gusts of wind whistling around the mountainside. We would hear it coming before it actually hit our cotton tent on this sloping, snowy ledge, and Tenzing and I were inside and it seemed to us that the main thing holding the tent down was our weight. We didn't know anything about windchill factor in those days, but the windchill factor must have been very considerable. And I really felt that night, with the wind blowing as it was, that we might have trouble with the summit. I have never been the sort of person who is absolutely confident that he is going to reach the summit of any mountain. I was always very much aware of the fact that weather conditions or snow conditions could make getting to the summit difficult or even impossible.

But early in the morning the wind eased off. There was still wind all the way up, but it wasn't anywhere near as severe. I looked out of the tent about 4:30 in the morning, and there were clouds around, but it was a good deal clearer, so I realized that we had a good chance to put in a push towards the summit.

I was absolutely certain that Tenzing and I could do this. Tenzing was keen to go. We knew that the conditions were good enough, so we just made our preparations and pushed on.

I wouldn't say the final push was fun. It was jolly hard work, actually, and the long slope up to the South Summit had soft snow, and we were very concerned about the potential avalanche.

Royal Geographical Society

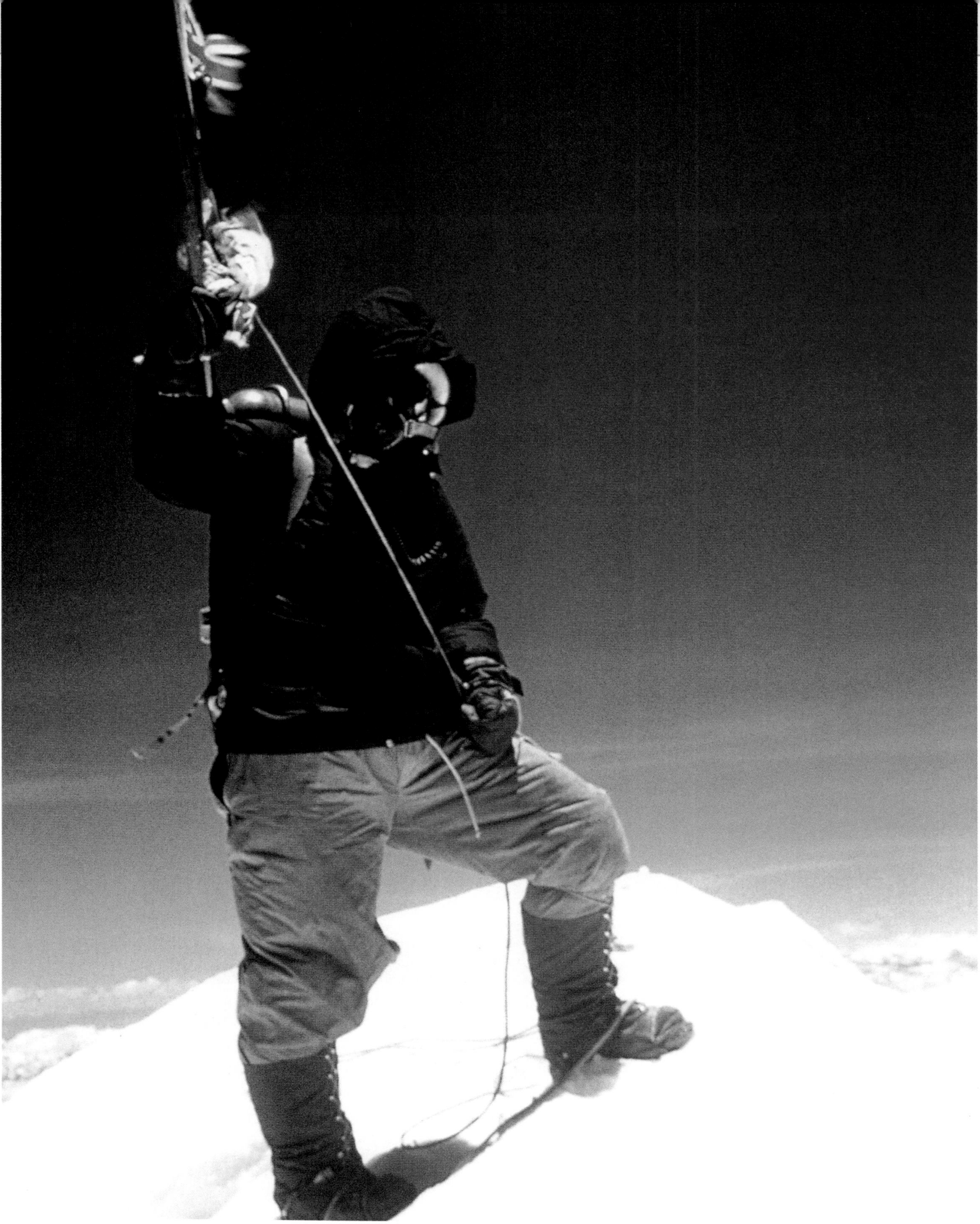

Sir Edmund Hillary/Royal Geographical Society

But, you know, as I've said many times, this was Everest, so we felt we had to push it a bit harder than maybe we would ordinarily.

Once we climbed that step on the ridge, which is now called the Hillary Step, the ridge sort of ran away, almost out of sight. You couldn't really see exactly where the top was. We couldn't find the summit. It wasn't until we came to a place where we could see that the ridge ahead dropped away, and we could see Tibet in front of us, that I realized we must be pretty close to the summit. Up above us the snow rounded off into a dome, and we realized that that must be the top. It's not a really sharp summit—the sort you hold your hands around. It's a summit that you can stand on reasonably comfortably. Six or eight people could probably all stand together. A nice summit.

I took my oxygen off and took photographs down all the leading ridges, just to make sure I had plenty of evidence that we had actually got to

Hillary took this picture facing east from the summit. Makalu (right), a 27,766-foot peak, had yet to be climbed. Eighty miles distant were the peaks of the Kangchenjunga massif (left), which rose as high as 28,169 feet.

the top. Then I looked across at Makalu and I can remember assessing the routes up Makalu, which hadn't yet been climbed. I began mentally working out a potential route to the summit, which was actually the route by which it was finally climbed.

You never stopped working.

No, even on top of Everest, I was still looking at other mountains and thinking of how one might climb them.

When we got to the top, I didn't really have a tremendous feeling of ecstasy or joy. I didn't leap around or throw my hands in the air or something. We were tired, of course, and I was very much aware of the fact that we had to get safely down the mountain again. I think my major feeling was one of satisfaction, I really did have a feeling of "Well, we've finally made it." I know I had a little feeling almost of surprise, too, because there had been a lot of other very good expedition

Scenes from Camp IV: Having "knocked the bastard off," Hillary (right, at left) was elated but tired as he trudged into camp. Going up and coming down, he and Norgay drank hot tea with lemon to rehydrate.

attempts at Everest, and they had not been able to get to the top, and here finally Tenzing and I were there. I certainly didn't have an arrogant feeling.

Before we came down off the mountain, Lowe met us on the South Col. He said, "How did it go?" And I said, "Well, George, we knocked the bastard off."

When you got down, everything got crazy quickly. The knighthood came through almost immediately.

I had nothing to do with that.

You didn't want it?

If I'd been given the choice, I wouldn't have had it, no.

Why is that?

Well, I didn't really think I was the right material for a knighthood, and it had never been something that I had any ambition to have. But I found in later years that if you're philosophical about it, it really can be quite useful in a way— useful for getting support for other activities.

And then there was all that confusion about Tenzing getting on top first.

When we got back to Kathmandu Valley, we were met by communists—there was quite a strong communist movement on the mountain and in the villages. Now, I'm not anticommunist by any manner or means, but there was no question they felt that it was most important that they should stress that Tenzing had got to the summit first. Whereas to the ordinary mountaineer, of course, it's a matter of complete indifference. So they got Tenzing aside, and they really batted away at him, and I think they frightened him to death, quite frankly. And he, even though he couldn't at that stage read or write, signed a document that they presented to him, which indicated he had got to the top first. As he said afterwards, he had no idea what he was signing. It really was quite an uncomfortable time. In the end, Tenzing and I agreed that he did not get to the top first, and we agreed that we would say that we reached the summit together. That is basically what happened. Who actually set foot there first is a matter of complete indifference. But people still ask me the question.

Your life changed profoundly.

It was certainly the occasion that brought me to public notice. The media created a Hillary and Tenzing that really didn't exist. They made us into heroic figures, and it didn't really matter what we thought or said or did.

The main thing was that as long as I didn't believe all this rubbish that was written, I would be O.K. I never did believe it. And I think I've survived reasonably well. I never deny the fact that I think I did pretty well on Everest. On the other hand, never for a moment have I ever suggested that I was the heroic figure that the

By the time they reached Kathmandu, Norgay and Hillary were world famous. Norgay immediately messaged his family: "Myself along with one Sahib reached summit Everest on 29th May. Hope you will feel happy."

New Studio—Kathmandu

media and the public were making me out to be. The public really like heroic figures that they can look on with great admiration, and whether it's true or not doesn't seem terribly important.

Were you stunned by the reception?

No. George and I actually thought it was a bit of a scream. We all went to Britain and there was a tremendous reaction. I can remember walking across the street and a London taxi stopped and the taxi driver—he was a tough-looking cookie—came out and said, "You're Hillary, aren't you?" And I said, "Yeah." And he said, "Congratulations. You know, you've done a great job for us!" He got back in his cab and drove off. Now, the contrast was when we arrived back here in New Zealand.

In New Zealand (above), Hillary was every kid's hero. In England (left) he got a title and endless acclaim, while fellow Kiwi George Lowe got a nice medal.

Hulton Getty/Liaison Agency

There was a big crowd—Mayor of Auckland and all the rest of it. I was put in this great big limousine to be driven off, and the window was down and a big hefty farmer-looking type thrust his hand in, grabbed me and shook me by the hand and said, "Good on you, Ed!" He said, "You did very well for yourself." Completely different. In England they thanked me for all we had done for Britain, but over here, in rather New Zealand fashion, they complimented me for having done well for myself.

It never really let up. How do you feel when you go down to the grocery store and pass a five-dollar note with your picture on it?

I don't spend a great deal of time thinking about that sort of thing.

You never stopped adventuring.

As far as I was concerned, the climb at Mount Everest really was a beginning rather than an end. It gave me the opportunity to do lots of interesting things.

Five years after the Everest expedition, Hillary realized another dream by reaching the South Pole. At latitude 90 degrees south he shook hands with the English geologist Sir Vivian Fuchs.

You speedboated down the Ganges, you climbed Mount Herschel on Antarctica, you went on that three-year tractor expedition to the South Pole. What was the allure of Antarctica?

It was a very good challenge. Vivian Fuchs wanted to cross the Antarctic and carry out the task that [Ernest] Shackleton had tried. He invited me on the expedition, I think mainly because he felt that would enable him to get support from the government. It was a good challenge. And it was snow and ice, which I enjoy.

Was it harder than Everest?

Oh, no. It was very different in many ways. The problems of snow and ice were similar, but on a big mountain like Everest, there were more immediate dangers—the possibility of avalanche or falling off the mountain or going down a crevasse. In the Antarctic, the temperatures on the whole were colder, the distances were vast and it was a much longer sort of business, really. So in our trip to the South Pole, we were under

In 1960, Hillary received a petition from a Sherpa asking for another school. He was careful that his institutions didn't trample the cultural or religious life of the community, and proud that most graduates stayed in their villages after receiving an education.

constant tension, for long, long periods. For hours we'd be under great tension. Whereas on a big mountain it would be for short periods.

I enjoyed it. I had been keen to get to the South Pole.

And while you were doing the adventures, you became involved with Nepal, building the schools and so on.

I had built up a very close friendship with the Sherpa people, and it was obvious that they lacked so many of the things that we took for granted—there were no schools, and certainly no medical attention available. I liked the Sherpas and I admired them and I just thought, well, maybe there's something I can do. Once I've decided to do something, I do usually try to carry it through to fruition. So once the Sherpas said that the main thing they wanted was a school, I was determined that I would raise the funds. So we went ahead and built a school and hospital in 1966. We now have 30 schools and a couple of hospitals and a dozen medical clinics.

And you became a diplomat as well as a school builder.

I became the New Zealand ambassador to India—high commissioner, as we call it—and I was also high commissioner to Bangladesh and ambassador to Nepal.

We had four and a half years in Delhi [from 1985 to '89] and we really enjoyed it. June and I on many occasions were invited along to quite important functions in which we would be the only foreigners, and we loved that. I like India, it's a really interesting place. I think it's doing very much better. When I first went to India in 1951, India was very different—much greater poverty, dead people in the streets. Now that's very rare.

But along the way there was tragedy. Tell us about Louise Rose.

I married Louise shortly after the Everest expedition. Louise was a good deal younger than I was, but she was a keen mountaineer. She was very much involved in the out-of-doors, and was lots of fun. We did a lot of family treks, we really enjoyed them. They weren't really extreme, they were more camping trips, but pretty energetic trekking. We were very keen that the kids should learn to enjoy the out-of-doors, enjoy swimming and camping and walking around the

hills and all the rest of it. But I never at any stage really tried to persuade them—even Peter—to become a mountaineer.

And then Louise and your daughter Belinda were killed in Nepal in 1975. It must have been awfully hard to recover from that.

Well, of course it was tremendously difficult. It changed everything. My life disappeared, and I did drift for a time. I didn't really believe that time would heal the loss. But after five or six years, I found I was getting interested in some new things. Time did heal things. But things have always remained different.

What did you think of Peter's continuing to climb?

That was entirely up to him. He decided he wanted to do it and he went off. I've never climbed with Peter on a big mountain. He did more and more of it and became surer, a much better technical climber than ever I was. He was

Sir Edmund and Louise ventured out often with the children, Peter, Belinda and Sarah, to locations from a Virginia campground to the Australian desert to a glacier at 17,000 feet in Nepal.

UPI/Corbis-Bettmann

Scott Fischer/Woodfin Camp

pleased me was: He complimented me on the Hillary Step. He said it was more demanding than he expected it to be.

What about all the climbing traffic on Everest these days?

Well, I've been sort of fairly outspoken on this. I think, A, that too many people have been permitted to go on the mountain at one time and, B, that there's too much rubbish being left on the mountain.

The commercialized trips and the overcrowding were what caused the tragedy [in 1996, when eight died on Everest after summiting late and getting caught in an afternoon storm—the incident chronicled in Jon Krakauer's *Into Thin Air,* among other books]. It was inevitable. I've been forecasting a disaster of that nature for some time. And it will happen again. You see, with so many climbers on the mountain, climbers are practically queuing up for the difficult parts. What happens then, quite a few don't get to the top till three or later in the afternoon. And then, like in this instance, the late weather comes sweeping in.

Are the leaders of these guided expeditions sufficiently talented?

They're usually pretty competent. But the climbers are certainly not as competent. I met one of Hall's groups. [New Zealander Rob Hall, a commercial guide, died in the 1996 storm at 28,700 feet, along with a client, an American named Doug Hansen.] One of Hall's clients told me that he'd never been on a mountain. But he had paid his $65,000—or whatever—and felt he was going to be taken to the top and back safely for that money.

You could tell he was a poor climber?

He told us he wasn't a good climber.

What did Hall say when you asked him about taking such a guy up?

Rob Hall was a firm believer in the fact that he could get them up and down safely.

Did this thinking get Hall killed?

Well, I'm sure if he had been on Everest with a serious expedition, he'd have got himself off. But . . . who was that man with Hall?

Hansen.

Hansen. Now, apparently Hansen had been on the mountain the previous year and had got quite

always trying difficult routes, wasn't interested in climbing easy routes. He had quite a few accidents. He nearly killed himself once, and I think four members of his parties died on the mountains. So I felt relieved when he finally did climb Everest. It was up the same route we had used. He telephoned me from the summit of the mountain, quite an unusual experience.

What did you talk about?

Oh, we talked about all sorts of things. We had a very good discussion. One thing that rather

On the fateful day in 1996, climbers—some of whom wouldn't return—lined up for the summit. In recent years as many as 40 people have reached the top in a single day.

high. But he couldn't handle the atmosphere well and was lucky he got off. To take a man who had had trouble back up a year later is taking a very big risk, a considerable chance indeed.

What was your reaction when you first learned of the tragedy?

While I expected it, I was obviously shaken. We actually heard a man dying on the mountain, talking to his wife as he was dying. [Hall had been patched through from just below the summit, and a tape recording of the telephone conversation was made.] This was very dramatic, very sad stuff.

My own personal feeling—I would have preferred to die peacefully alone and let the world find out about it later.

You say you expect it to happen again. Can anything be done to prevent such occurrences in the future?

Well, I certainly put some responsibility [for the tragedy] on the Nepalese government. I think they should allow only two or three expeditions a year. But I'll bet you they don't do it. To them, the money's too important. They have said they would reduce the number of expeditions and increase the cost to go on the mountain. Now, I don't agree with the vast sum because it makes it become essentially only a sport for the wealthy or the extremely well sponsored. On the other hand, I do agree with them cutting down on expeditions—but I'll bet you they don't do it.

Has the nature of mountaineering itself changed, and if so, does this add to the danger too?

There has been an erosion of mountaineering values. It used to be a team effort. Nowadays, it's much too everybody-for-himself. Tenzing and I got to the top together, it wasn't first one, then the other. Now it's every man for himself. Not much you can do about it. That's the way people are these days.

With a traffic jam on top of the mountain, can these climbers possibly get the same kind of joy out of summiting that once was available—that was available to you?

I don't think they do get the same type of joy. I think we were the lucky ones, really. We had to do everything, we had to establish the route, we had to carry the gear up, we had to pioneer upper parts of the mountain. So we were really, in many ways, the fortunate ones. I mean, those sorts of challenges simply don't exist anymore.

You were born at the right time for what you wanted to do.

We were born at the right time.

Do you still go walking?

Almost every day. June's a keen walker, and we have a route here in Auckland that we do. And we have two cabins, one in the bush and one near the shore. I love to go walking there. I still love to go out.

John Van Hasselt/Sygma

Sir Edmund spends time at home in Auckland, in the New Zealand bush or at the beach, and several months each year in the Himalayas, looking after the schools and hospitals.

Alone in Thin Air

Reinhold Messner (2)

Reinhold Messner, an Italian mountaineer, changed all the rules on Everest.

He recalled the experience vividly: "I am standing on the highest point on Earth . . . I still don't know how I have made it but I know that I can't do any more . . . I am not only as heavy as a corpse, I am incapable of taking anything in. I cannot distinguish above and below."

It was August 20, 1980, and 36-year-old Reinhold Messner, already a legendary mountaineer, had just accomplished what would be regarded as the greatest climbing feat of the modern age. He had conquered Everest alone, by what he called "fair means."

Himalayan Sherpas, for their part, had long used the term "English air" for the oxygen that Western climbers lugged up the slopes in tanks. The natives had developed a high regard for Messner and his

In 1980, Messner was like a fly on the north side of Everest as he went, solo and without oxygen, to the top. Following this climb, there were no successful expeditions on the North Face for four years, though seven attempts were mounted.

partner, Peter Habeler, when in 1978 those two men became the first to summit on Everest "without oxygen." Now, two years later, during the height of the monsoon season, fully aware of the ravaging effects of oxygen deprivation, Messner was back on the 29,028-foot mountain—carrying a 44-pound backpack and traveling solo.

His girlfriend, Nena Holguin, was just beneath the Tibetan North Face. Except for her and Messner, there was no one else on the mountain. (They had been accompanied to the foot of the mountain by an interpreter and a liaison.) Messner felt this aloneness keenly in the predawn darkness, shortly after he began his ascent. He slipped and found himself free-falling into a gaping crevasse. He was tethered to no one; he was so very much on his own. Suddenly, he struck a snow bridge that was suspended between the walls of what might easily have been his tomb, and his fall was broken. "The sweat of fear breaks from all my pores, covers my body with a touch which is as icy as the iridescent blue-green ice walls between which I am imprisoned." Carrying no radio or ropes, crampons still tucked in his pack, Messner swore—promising the Fates, promising himself—that he would turn back if he could

On the solo ascent (above, at the summit, and right), Messner lugged a rucksack containing a bivouac tent, a sleeping bag and a plastic mattress. His food included strips of beef, dried fruit, chocolate, sardines, tomato soup and Tibetan salt tea. He carried a camera that could be attached to his lightweight titanium ice ax, and thus he could photograph himself while climbing.

The Air Up There

At the top of Everest, atmospheric pressure is 33 percent that at sea level. Mountaineers who summit find 66 percent less oxygen available for breathing. That's not enough air to burn kerosene, not enough for a helicopter to take flight (which has obvious consequences for high-altitude rescue operations). For some people, it would be not enough to live.

"What makes Everest so dangerous is not the steepness of its flanks, nor the sheer masses of rock and ice that can break off without warning; what is far worse is the reduced air pressure in its upper regions," Reinhold Messner wrote in *Climbing* magazine in September 1999. "This saps your judgment and strength, even your ability to feel anything at all. That's what makes you so vulnerable and afraid up there."

Many climbers begin to feel the effects of altitude at approximately 8,000 feet, with symptoms of what is called acute mountain sickness—headache, nausea, general weakness. At 12,000 feet and above, high altitude pulmonary edema (fluid filling the lungs) and high altitude cerebral edema (fluid accumulating in the brain) are ever-present risks. Either can be deadly if not recognized and remedied with a quick retreat to lower ground.

As Messner indicates, altitude sickness in its various forms can take down even the fittest of climbers. It strikes most commonly during a too-rapid ascent. Acclimatizing—limiting climbing to 2,000 feet a day and drinking large quantities of water each day—allows the human body to adapt to the stresses encountered at high altitudes. One way to understand the need for acclimatization is to consider: Were you flown to the top of Everest and dropped off, you would die within the hour.

Alpine Club Collection

The Australian George Finch (left) was the best climber on the 1922 British Everest expedition. Some colleagues, including George Mallory, thought the use of supplemental oxygen was unnecessary. But in the event, Finch performed better than they did at altitude, and a tradition was established.

A native son of the South Tyrol in Italy, Messner trained at home for each of his more than 3,000 trips into the mountains.

negotiate his way out. He made a pledge that was painful: "I will give up."

Stars shining overhead, Messner flipped on his headlamp and saw a ramp leading up the 26 feet he had fallen. Within minutes he was out. Within moments, he had broken his word and was headed up the mountain.

Six years later, Messner became the first person to have climbed the world's 14 highest mountains, each more than 26,250 feet high. "Messner is to climbing what Michael Jordan is to basketball," Jon Krakauer, author of *Into Thin Air,* wrote in *Outside* magazine. "He has taken the sport to a level not previously imagined." And then he changed course, opting in the late 1980s for the lowlands and long polar treks. In 1989–90 he crossed Antarctica on skis in 92 days. In 1993 he and his brother Hubert crossed Greenland, also on skis. In 1995 the Messners attempted a round-trip walk to the North Pole but had to abort when the ice collapsed and supplies were lost. Reinhold Messner spent the last years of the past century questing in Asia after the fabled Yeti—a suitable mission, with one storied, near legendary mountain animal tracking another.

In the Footsteps of Peary and Amundsen

Will Steger is a throwback, and a trailblazer.

Gordon Wiltsie

I used to teach at a canoeing camp on the next lake," recalled Judy Spansberger of Ely, Minn. "One day there was this really skinny, grungy little guy with hair down to the middle of his back—he was pretty unwashed. He was using the pay phone at the camp. I asked someone, 'Who's that?' and they said, 'Will Steger. He's kind of a different guy, quiet. Lives in a cabin near here and comes over to use the phone.' Back then, Will was just another broke hippie, like all of us."

In fact, in the early 1980s, Will Steger was a former science teacher from a St. Paul suburb who had thrown his savings into a 220-acre North Woods par-

cel of land and was trying to figure out what was next. He had 100,000 miles of hitchhiking behind him, and a few minor-league adventures—a boat trip down the Mississippi with his brother, a kayaking escapade on the Yukon River—which were noteworthy only in that they had convinced him he was most alive in the wild.

"I put my kayak into the Yukon and felt a cold thrill," Steger once recounted. "That was my first taste of what the wilderness is. It's frightening, uncomfortable, lonely. You wish you were home, but it leaves an indelible mark."

Steger began raising sled dogs on his land. He

Steger initially went to the North Pole via dogsled in 1986 (opposite). He then returned in 1995 leading a team that pulled its own weight for much of the trip (above).

Per Breiehagen/Adventure Photo & Film

Jim Brandenburg/NGS Image Collection

trekked in Canada and then Greenland. The next step came to him in an epiphany: "I had always been going north, and the ultimate extension of that is the North Pole. One day I was stuck in a storm in the Canadian Barren Grounds. The wind was hitting the tent at 70 miles an hour, and it was freezing. At that moment it came to me what a *pure* trip to the Pole should be: Go with a team of dogs and make it unsupported, without resupply. You see, when Peary got there, he built way stations across the Arctic ice and kept having food and fresh dogs sent up to him at the front. Then he made his dash from about a hundred miles out. I wanted to go the whole way with one team of dogs and all our food. It's seldom that you perceive an ultimate challenge. I felt that I was the right person at the right time—

A dog's life is a tough one if its master is Will Steger. The sled dogs that dug in against the Antarctic cold (above) didn't face the danger of open ocean that Steger's North Pole team did. In 1986 the expedition fished its dogs from the sea more than once (right).

perhaps in all of history—to do this thing."

A half million dollars of sponsorship funds and three years of planning and training later, Steger did it. On March 8, 1986, seven men, one woman and 49 Arctic huskies and Canadian Eskimo dogs set off from Canada's Ellesmere Island determined, as Steger defined it, to be the first "to reach the Pole

by manual navigation alone, and by the power and perseverance of ourselves and our sled dogs."

Steger, 41 at the time, and his expedition coleader, fellow Minnesotan Paul Schurke, had carefully selected teammates who had the ability to thrive in one of the harshest and starkest landscapes on earth. They had chosen well, and the unit worked together efficiently as it traveled over the ice during the period from March, when the sun first shines on the Arctic Circle, to May, when the spring thaw of the Arctic Ocean breaks up the ice. The team never flagged as it endured temperatures that fell to as low as –68° F, raging storms, surging 60-to-100-foot pressure ridges of ice and the grueling task

In a place barren of creature comforts, everyday tasks were ordeals. In Antarctica, an al fresco lunch break was cold business. Colder were Victor Boyarsky's morning snow baths (right).

of lugging more than three tons of supplies.

The expedition did not pass the halfway point until April 16, far behind schedule. "Paul and I discussed making a two-man dash for it, and we presented this option to the team," Steger admitted later. But the team took the news badly, and Steger and Schurke abandoned the idea. In midspring, leads, or breaks in the ice, began to open, and the adventurers had to spend hours searching for ice bridges. They stepped gingerly and hopefully onto floating ice floes, which they used as ferries to cross swaths of cold, black water. Each day, they were traveling for at least 10 hours and eating 7,000 fat-laden calories.

Two members of the team had to be evacuated, one with cracked ribs, another with frostbite. Several dogs, too, were airlifted out. As their load lightened, the remaining members went from five sleds to three and dumped 300 pounds of gear. At one point the smaller team zoomed 80 miles in four days. The final week was frantic. Steger, already severely frostbitten, caught a virus and couldn't eat. The sun was now opening leads in the ice every day. Expedition member Ann E. Bancroft had to be pulled from the Arctic waters at one point, Steger himself at another.

Finally, on May 2, after 56 days of travel, six members of the Steger International Polar Expedition became the first to successfully dogsled to the North Pole without having to rely on renewed supplies. They unfurled a banner with the word PEACE

Will Steger/NGS Image Collection

Jim Brandenburg/Minden Pictures (2)

emblazoned across it; the erstwhile hippie Steger smiled broadly. Bancroft, the first woman to reach the North Pole, read a declaration from the team: "As we, six adventurers from different parts of the world, stand here where the lines of longitude of all countries meet, we believe this journey stands for hope—hope that other seemingly impossible goals can be met by people everywhere."

Steger was not done: There would be other major expeditions. From July 1989 to March 1990, the Minnesotan led an international team of six men on a 3,741-mile dogsled expedition across Antarctica. This had been Ernest Shackleton's dream: to traverse the frozen continent on foot. In 1995, Steger's International Arctic Project, another dogsled venture, became the first to cross the Arctic from Russia to Canada via the Pole in a single season.

And then, simplifying his life in the new millennium, Steger scaled back, returning to his land by the lake in the North Woods. The Antarctica trip cost $11 million. "That's what big-time adventuring is about these days," Steger said. "We need food, we need flights, we need a command boat in the ocean for seven months. That costs money. The problem is, it puts a lot of pressure on us.

"I'll tell you very honestly, I preferred it before—solo, no radio, just out there alone."

Adventuring in the new age: Newscasters flew to the North Pole to report Steger's arrival in 1986 (above). Expeditions aren't necessarily nationalistic efforts anymore, and members of the team had both U.S. and Canadian flags to plant. To complete the ceremonies (right), Bancroft read her eloquent declaration.

Where No Man Had Gone Before

Lynn Hill plotted a bold new course in rock climbing.

For three decades the world's top free-climbers wondered about the Nose, a 3,000-foot sheer wall on the granite monolith called El Capitan in California's Yosemite National Park. They stood there and considered the Nose the way that Mallory had looked at Everest. Could it be done? Would it be done? Most of the climbers who gazed upward were men, but among them was Lynn Hill, and no one was discounting her chances.

Born in 1961 in Fullerton, Calif., she was an athletic little girl who grew to be a monster athlete of a woman. She won television's *Survival of the Fittest* competition four times in a row, and by the late 1980s, Hill was winning every rock-climbing competition that she entered.

Not content to be an ordinary nuts-and-bolts climber, she dedicated herself to free-climbing—ascending without protective hardware for handholds

In 1988, Hill trained for her El Cap assault on the sheer rock faces of New York's Shawangunk Mountains.

Hill knew the Nose like the palm of her hand, having scouted it in stages (left). At Cinque Torre in Italy's Dolomites, she hung out on a 5.13 route (above).

or rest spots. This is the pure form of rock climbing and obviously the more difficult and dangerous. Gaining tentative purchase on "ledges" that were no more than ripples in the rock, she would reach hand over hand until she stood atop the mountain. In 1990 the French climber Jean-Baptiste Tribout challenged her, insisting that no woman could successfully climb "a five-one-four" (rock-climbing routes are rated in degrees of difficulty from 5.0 to 5.14d). Hill, five foot two and 100 pounds, went to Tribout's backyard and knocked off the 5.14a Masse Critique in Cimai, France.

Challenges, TV contests, competitions (she has won more than 30 international events): These were fun, but were they adventuresome? Where was the breakthrough? How could she take her game to a new level?

In 1993, Hill chalked up and took her shot at the Nose. The climb required three and a half days, but she made it to the top, proving it could be done. A year later she returned to El Cap and spidered up the wall again—this time in 23 hours. That is still regarded as the greatest rock-climbing accomplishment ever. No one has come close to doing that route faster—and no one, Monsieur Tribout, includes men.

Air

The Lindbergh Flight, 1927

The Fliers

The brothers **Wilbur** and **Orville Wright** take to the skies.

I don't think men will fly for a thousand years," Wilbur Wright predicted in 1901, shortly after testing a glider that he and his brother had built. Well, Wright was wrong.

He and his brother Orville were the proprietors of a bicycle shop in Dayton, Ohio, but it was their interest in aviation rather than cycling that would grow into an obsession. As early as the mid-1890s they were reading everything they could about the prospects for flight.

They were diligent, smart students, not to mention talented engineers and mechanics. One day, observing buzzards in flight, the brothers agreed that the birds were changing the angle of their wings to balance in a shifting wind. It looked like a clue.

By 1899 the Wright brothers were putting their

The Wrights began testing gliders in 1900, and in 1902, Wilbur piloted their latest model over Kill Devil Hills, N.C. (right). By then their aircraft had gained a rear rudder (above). Despite the history in the making, the brothers progressed largely in private.

notion to work, building kites with movable wing-tips. In their gliders, which they began building the following year, control wires were connected from the pilot's position out to the wings. In the summer of 1901, the Wrights put their glider through hundreds of trials over sand dunes near Kitty Hawk, N.C. The reason Wilbur spoke so pessimistically about the future of manned flight was that the glider could never be kept aloft longer than a few minutes per day—total.

Library of Congress

Smithsonian Institution

December 1903: Wilbur (above) crashed shortly after takeoff, then it was Orville's turn. He opened the throttle of the 12-horsepower engine and felt the *Flyer* lift off its launching rail. He averaged a speed of 10 feet per second during a flight of 12 seconds.

According to one family member, Wilbur was ready to give up entirely. Orville, the optimist, urged his brother to stick with it. Back in the bike shop, the Wrights constructed wind tunnels and tested more than 200 different wing shapes. With a new wing and the addition of a rear rudder, their 1902 glider made a record 622.5-foot flight.

Now for a motor. In 1903 the brothers built what they called simply the *Flyer*. It was a 600-pound plane made of wood, muslin and wire. It sported two propellers and a four-cylinder engine. That September, Orville, 32, and Wilbur, 36, returned to Kill Devil Hills near Kitty Hawk, one of the windiest places in the country, lugging their craft 800 miles to its meeting with history.

The Wrights, adventurous men as well as inquisitive engineers, did their own flying. They were pioneers but not daredevils, careful not to put a thing aloft before they thought it truly ready. "I do not intend to take dangerous chances," Wilbur wrote to his father, "both because I have no wish to get hurt and because a fall would stop my experimenting, which I would not like at all." By December, the Wrights were confident they had a device that was ready to fly. Wilbur's attempt on the 14th failed, and on the 17th it was Orville's turn. He climbed into

the wild-looking flying machine. Rube Goldberg wasn't drawing his contraptions yet, but had he been, his sketches might have looked like the Wrights'. Orville lay facedown, his hips resting on a wooden cradle. By shifting his hips from one side to the other, he could tug on wires connecting the cradle to both the wingtips and rudders.

After a preflight check, Orville released a wire that restrained the *Flyer* on its 60-foot wood-and-metal track. Wilbur gripped a wingtip to steady the machine as it accelerated. He ran alongside the airplane like a father guiding a son on a first bicycle attempt. The *Flyer* powered down the track, picking up speed and plowing into the gusty 27 mph headwind. At seven mph, it took off. The *Flyer* dipped, then rose to 12 feet, dipped again, rose again. It flew 50 feet . . . 80 . . . 120 feet!

And then, with "a sudden dart," it fell.

"They done it!" called out Johnny Moore, a local who witnessed the event. "Damned if they ain't flew!" The flight had lasted only 12 seconds and covered but 120 feet—less than the wingspan of a 747—but the Wrights had, in fact, done it. They had lived one of mankind's longest-held dreams: They had flown. They had succeeded in taking a heavier-than-air machine into the skies in a self-propelled, sustained and controlled flight.

The Wright brothers completed three more flights that first day, the longest of them lasting 59 seconds and traveling 852 feet. Suddenly the future, which had looked so bleak and unpromising to Wilbur, was boundless.

Having pioneered powered flight, the Wrights (above, Orville at left, in 1909) were not done. They kept refining their *Flyer,* showing off and then selling new models. In 1909, the latest edition performed banked turns at the first international air show, in Reims, France (right). Not all demonstrations were successful. In 1908, Orville crashed while trying to prove the *Flyer*'s mettle to the U.S. Army. His passenger, Lt. Thomas Selfridge, was killed— the world's first airplane fatality.

The Enigma

Richard E. Byrd accomplished much. But how much?

Richard Evelyn Byrd was navigating, Floyd Bennett piloting, when Byrd peered through the cabin window and saw a bad leak in the oil tank of the starboard motor. He pointed it out to Bennett, who wrote a note for Byrd to read: THAT MOTOR WILL STOP. He suggested landing on the Arctic ice cap to fix the leak. Byrd thought that too dangerous and made the decision to fly on.

That much is not in dispute. But did Byrd and Bennett press for the North Pole, covering a 1,350-mile round-trip in 15½ hours, or did they turn back toward Norway well short of their goal? Byrd wrote in *Exploring with Byrd* that "the prize was actually

In New Jersey, Byrd made final preparations (opposite), then headed for the Arctic, where he reconnoitered with Bennett (above, right). On May 9, 1926, the two men took off (left) from Spitsbergen, Norway, bound for the Pole.

Amundsen (left, foreground) watched as Byrd and Bennett's plane returned; his own hopes of being first over the Pole seemed, at that moment, dashed. Byrd was comfortable accepting the acclaim of an adoring nation, manifested above in a parade up New York City's Broadway.

in sight. We could not turn back. At 9:02 a.m., May 9, 1926, Greenwich civil time, our calculations showed us to be at the Pole! The dream of a lifetime had at last been realized."

But according to very different writing discovered in 1996—in a flight diary that had been kept by Byrd—the commander was so concerned about the fuel leak that he turned the plane around when it was still shy of the Pole by 150 miles. If the diary holds the truth, then a trio including peripatetic adventurer Roald Amundsen of Norway made the first flight over the North Pole when, on May 12—three days after Byrd and Bennett's attempt—they sailed directly above latitude 90 degrees north in a dirigible.

The controversy surrounding Byrd's North Pole mission points up just how large a role ego and glory played during the golden age of adventuring. Byrd, a Virginian of privilege, an educated youth

Working in –60°F temperatures in the '30s, Byrd's Antarctic team built an igloo hangar (above). Three 65-foot radio towers rose above Little America.

who had seen the world by the age of 12, a graduate of Annapolis, a distinguished officer in the U.S. Navy, was certainly considered an honorable man. At age 37 his record was pristine, and dignitaries and the American public were quick to lionize him for his feat. Byrd returned from the north a national hero, and he and Bennett were each awarded the Congressional Medal of Honor. It seems inconceivable that these two men of accomplishment could have watched Amundsen make his flight, could have accepted those medals, and could nonetheless have continued with their claim—knowing it to be false. But there it is, as implied in the diary: Byrd could not overcome his lust for glory.

It's impossible now to plumb Byrd's mind. But knowing what we know, it is fascinating to consider that he never flinched and in fact went on to a career of ever greater achievement and acclaim. He helped Charles Lindbergh with preparations for the 1927 transatlantic solo flight that would bring Lucky Lindy phenomenal fame. Shortly thereafter, Byrd and three others flew the Atlantic from west to east. When asked by none other than Amundsen how he would follow up his North Pole flight, Byrd answered boldly, "Fly over the South Pole"—and he did so, indisputably, on November 29, 1929. He was soon promoted to rear admiral.

His explorations on and above the frozen continent, where he served as commander of the U.S. Antarctic Service from 1939 at Franklin Delano Roosevelt's behest, were extraordinary. Many adventurers pay lip service to the idea of science and

In 1934, Byrd spent the winter at a one-man weather station (above), 123 miles from Little America, nearly dying of carbon monoxide poisoning. In 1947 the image-conscious admiral returned for a photo op.

research in the field—they're really after the thrill of the chase—but Byrd's Highjump and Deep Freeze operations on Antarctica greatly increased our knowledge of that barren place, while setting standards for polar research to follow. Commanding as many as 4,200 men in extreme climatic conditions while demonstrating the importance of airplanes, radio communication and aerial photography in polar research, Byrd proved himself a great leader and innovator.

And in 1957 he died, in Boston, at age 68—perhaps thinking that all his secrets were safe with him.

A handsome, modest midwesterner, Lindbergh attended the University of Wisconsin for little more than a year before an interest in aviation prompted him to enroll in flight school. He was 25 years old when he posed beside his plane at a Long Island airfield.

Lucky Lindy

Perhaps no adventurer in U.S. history reached **Charles Lindbergh**'s level of fame.

For the first time in my life," said Charles Lindbergh's mother, Evangeline, "I realize that Columbus also had a mother." What mom wouldn't have been concerned? Her only child was about to attempt a solo airplane crossing of the Atlantic, a challenge that had already left six people dead. Lindbergh's equipment seemed more suitable for a Boy Scout outing than a long-distance flight: Two fishhooks. Five meat sandwiches. One black rubber raft. A hunting knife, flares, string, flashlight, hacksaw blade. Forget the radio and parachute—much too heavy. Some people were saying he was nuts. His mother was worried silly.

In fact, Lindbergh, 25, was well positioned to make his nonstop, 3,610-mile flight from New York to Paris. His plane, the *Spirit of St. Louis,* had a state-of-the-art control panel, with an altimeter, a

tachometer, a temperature gauge and an Earth Inductor Compass system. The man, too, was prepared. As a mail courier, he had logged nearly 2,000 flight hours, negotiating treacherous weather, moonless nights and bailout landings. He had also spent 200 hours thrilling spectators as a wing-walker and parachutist. "I had been attracted to aviation by its adventure, not its safety, by the love of wind and height and wings," he said.

On May 20, 1927, Lindbergh settled into the wicker chair of his single-engine, 27-foot 9-inch airplane at Roosevelt Field on Long Island, N.Y. He revved the engine and the plane with its 3,000-pound load (much of it fuel) labored across the field, then lifted off, clearing the telephone wires by just 20 feet. Lindbergh headed north over New England, swept across Newfoundland and then pointed his plane out to sea.

The *Spirit* cut through thick fog and sleet, holding tight through bone-rattling turbulence. Lindbergh flew at 10,000 feet of altitude, at 10 feet of altitude, and at every altitude in between. He did this not only to avoid storms but to break the monotony, as sleep was a constant adversary. To stay awake, Lindbergh stuck his hand out the window and deflected air into his face. He tried resting one eye at a time. By the 16th hour, he was using his thumbs to pry open sagging eyelids, tensing his face muscles, stamping his feet. "How could I ever face

Lindbergh touched down in Europe at night, and he and his plane were feted by French President Gaston Doumergue at a banquet at the aerodrome. Lindbergh later wrote: "I was astonished at the effect my successful landing in France had on the nations of the world." The cheering was deafening and continuous as a victory tour moved on to Brussels and then London. There, his first attempt to land at Croydon Aerodrome had to be aborted when spectators swarmed the runway. The second try was successful (right).

my partners and say that I had failed to reach Paris because I was sleepy?" he said later. To spur himself on, he took to chanting: "There's no alternative but death and failure. No alternative but death and failure. No alternative but death and failure."

Twenty-eight hours after takeoff, Lindbergh caught a glimpse of fishing boats and the rugged coast of Ireland. "I know how the dead would feel to live again," he said to himself. When, four hours later, the coast of France came into view, he celebrated with a meat sandwich—the only food he ate during the entire flight.

Lindbergh circled the Eiffel Tower, and then, precisely 33 hours, 30 minutes and 29.9 seconds after leaving New York, he touched down safely at Le Bourget aerodrome.

Two weeks later, Lindbergh and the *Spirit of St. Louis* journeyed by boat to the United States, where 40 airplanes, two blimps and 4.5 million people—including Lindbergh's mother—gathered to greet the hero. It is hard to grasp the magnitude of Lindbergh's instant celebrity: He was not an overnight star, he was an overnight legend. And so, later, when the tragedies and mistakes of real life intruded—when his infant son was kidnapped and murdered, or when his acceptance of a German decoration in 1938 made him appear soft on Nazism—it seemed almost as if he were someone else, a separate Lindbergh, certainly not the Lucky Lindy of 1927. When he died in 1974, his golden moment was nearly half a century in the past, and America mourned a bygone age as much as it mourned the man.

In New York City, Lindbergh created a sensation (above). At a banquet there, former Secretary of State Charles Evans Hughes commented on the furor: "We measure heroes as we do ships, by their displacement. Colonel Lindbergh has displaced everything."

Earhart worked as a nurse in a military hospital in Canada during World War I and then as a social worker in Boston: There was no way to predict she would become a famous aviator, eventually piloting, in 1937, a "shiny new airplane," the twin-engine Lockheed Electra.

The Daredevil

She was **Amelia Earhart**, an iconic woman in life, an American legend in death.

Nothing scares Amelia," her sister Muriel said, and the words appear to be true. For after numerous crash landings, and knowing that 10 pilots had already died in the attempt, Amelia Earhart, in 1937, determined to become the first woman to fly around the world.

There were some who disagreed with Muriel, saying that Amelia wasn't necessarily fearless, merely reckless. Legend has it that as a child she steered her speeding sled between the legs of a galloping horse. In 1904, after returning from a family trip to the World's Fair in St. Louis, the seven-year-old designed and built a roller coaster in her Atchinson, Kans., backyard. When she was 23, she got $10 from her father and paid for a thrilling 10-minute flight at a local airfield. Right then Earhart decided she would be a flier, and later that day she announced the news. In her memoir, *The Fun of It,* she wrote: "'I think I'd like to fly,' I told the family casually that evening, knowing full well I'd die if I didn't."

In 1928, Earhart gained fame as the first woman to cross the Atlantic, but she was a passenger on that flight. To justify her reputation, she soloed four years later and landed in Northern Ireland, then hopped over to London where the Brits offered congratulations (below).

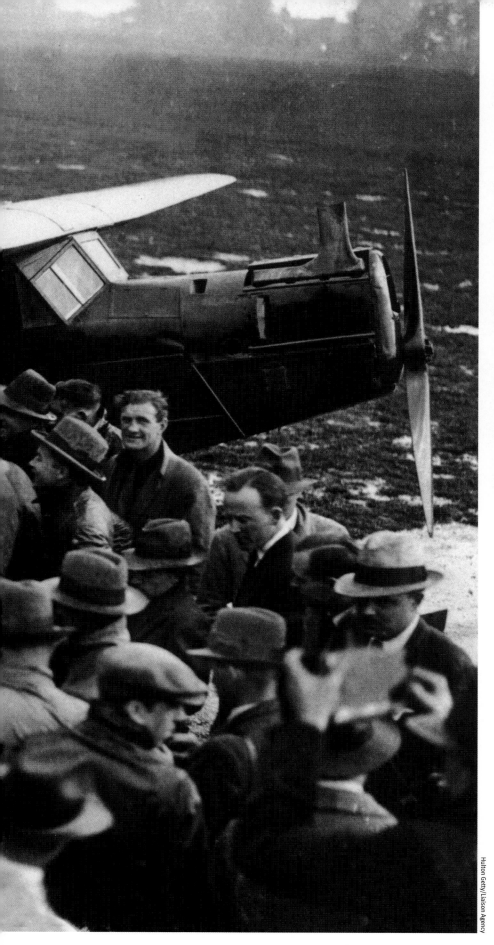

She again went to her dad, this time for $500 to purchase flying instruction. Miss Neta Snook, one of only a handful of women pilots and herself only 24, took Earhart under her wing in 1920—for a dollar a minute! Less than a year later, for $2,000, Earhart bought her first plane, a Kinner that she named *The Canary*.

Earhart quickly crashed her *Canary,* repaired it and set her first record by flying to 14,000 feet—higher than any woman before her. In 1928 she became the first woman to cross the Atlantic in an airplane. Four years later she made the crossing again, piloting solo, becoming the first woman to do that. She was almost killed on that trip when her Lockheed Vega went into a spin, hurtling toward "whitecaps too close for comfort" before she could pull the plane up. But Earhart survived the plummet and, 14 hours and 54 minutes after taking off from Newfoundland, she landed in Northern Ireland: Lady Lindy.

By the late 1930s, thanks to the PR efforts of her husband, George Palmer Putnam, and to her continuing successes—she was the first woman to solo

from Hawaii to California, and the first to go it alone across the United States—Earhart was a national hero. With her serene beauty and inherent charisma, she became a trendsetter in matters of style, as well as an early feminist icon.

In 1937 she told the *New York Herald Tribune* that she had "just one more good flight left in my system," and said she would become the first woman to fly around the world.

On her first attempt, Earhart completed the leg from Oakland to Honolulu, then crashed during the ensuing takeoff. One of her two navigators, Harry Manning, resigned, blaming the accident squarely on Earhart's lack of ability as a pilot. But Earhart was not deterred. On June 1, 1937, with an alcoholic Fred Noonan as her only navigator, she took off again, this time heading east. Amelia Earhart flew 22,000 miles—three quarters of the way around the world—before disappearing into clouds above the South Pacific. Her last words, as recorded by the ship *Itasca,* were, "WE MUST BE ON YOU BUT CANNOT SEE U BUT GAS IS RUNNING LOW BEEN UNABLE TO REACH YOU BY RADIO WE ARE FLYING AT ALTITUDE 1,000 FEET." She and Noonan had been headed for Howland Island, a speck of land barely two miles long. They didn't make it, and their airplane has never been found.

Earhart and Noonan were all smiles (above) as they checked their plotted route across the Pacific Ocean and, presumably, were in a similar frame of mind as they headed west over San Francisco's Golden Gate Bridge toward Honolulu during their first attempt to fly around the world.

No Barriers

Born with the right stuff, Chuck Yeager flew faster than the speed of sound.

Caption (left photo): **Yeager's bright orange X-1, a shade more than 30 feet long and with a 28-foot wingspan, was fueled by lethally combustible liquid oxygen and diluted ethyl alcohol.**

In six months of combat training in 1943, Chuck Yeager saw 13 comrades "auger in." Once stationed in Europe, he saw still more death. A self-proclaimed hillbilly who grew up hunting the hollers of West Virginia, Yeager was only 20 years old, and, at times, the losses "tore into your guts as if you'd been shot. Then there was nothing left to do but to go out and get blind drunk," he wrote in his 1985 autobiography, *Yeager*. "Those who couldn't put a lid on their grief . . . were either sent home or became a basket case."

Yeager put a lid on it and went on to fly 64 missions, shoot down 13 German aircraft and get shot down himself over France, escaping to safety by crossing the Pyrenees into Spain. It was policy to send a shot-down flier home, but Yeager refused the order. He went so far as to wangle a meeting with General Eisenhower, and finally the War Dept. relented, returning him to action. Of his 30-man squadron, he was one of three men to survive the war. "The secret of my success," wrote Yeager, "is that I always managed to live to fly another day."

The right stuff: That's what they called the kind of steel Chuck Yeager was made of. Born with 20/10 vision, an instinct for things mechanical and a steady hand that made him a hunting hero in his hometown of Hamlin, Yeager possessed, most crucially, an ability to put aside any fear of death. His focus was unwavering. Other fliers were in awe, and no one was surprised that it was Yeager, of more than 100 volunteer test pilots, who was selected by Col. Albert G. Boyd to break the sound barrier.

The barrier: This was the outside-the-envelope goal of a federally funded effort to understand high-speed flight, so as to improve aircraft design. Beyond the Mach 1 barrier was what Yeager called "the ugh-known." Theorists wondered if, at the speed of sound—760 mph at sea level, 660 mph at 40,000 feet—a wall of compressed air might not rip an air-

Air Force Photo

UPI/Corbis-Bettmann

Tucked under the massive B-29 bomber, the X-1 looked like an oversize gas tank (above). Although Yeager hitched a ride to altitude for the early sound-barrier tests, he eventually deployed the craft's landing gear (right) for a runway takeoff.

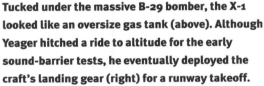

craft to shreds. Yeager, as his speeds increased, faced the same uncertainty Hillary had faced in the last steps up Everest, or Piccard as he dropped into the Marianas Trench: What would happen next?

During the tests in 1947, Yeager came to realize that if any plane could break the barrier, it would be the X-1, his model of which he named *Glamorous Glennis,* after his wife. Designed in the shape of a .50-caliber bullet, the plane was fast—and dangerous. There was no safe exit for its pilot, who, if he was able to bail out at all, would likely be shot back into a razor-sharp wing. If he was lucky enough to miss that, he would be ripped apart by the tail.

On test runs, the X-1 was cradled beneath a B-29 bomber and carried to 20,000 feet, where it was dropped into thin air. Then the pilot—Yeager— kicked into gear. He flew five tests in the X-1 before, at Mach .92, hitting a rough patch: "Like I was driving on bad shock absorbers over uneven paving stones." On his eighth flight, just shy of Mach 1, he lost control. He dumped his fuel, fought to harness the plane and somehow brought it down. Colonel

Boyd thought they had reached the end of the line. Jack Ridley, the X-1's engineer, thought otherwise.

On October 14, 1947, Yeager, with two cracked ribs from a wild horseback ride the day before, gingerly lowered himself out of the B-29's bomb bay and into the cockpit of *Glennis,* which had been slightly modified by Ridley. Yeager fired the engines yet again. At 42,000 feet he was shooting rocketlike toward the heavens; his speed was Mach .92. He kept climbing and reached Mach .98. The nee-

dle edged up farther and "then tipped right off the scale. We were flying supersonic! And it was smooth as a baby's bottom." The faster he went, the smoother the ride.

Yeager eventually flew the X-1 thirty-four times, reaching 1.45 Mach, or 957 miles per hour. *Glamorous Glennis* was put out to pasture at the Smithsonian Institution's aerospace museum in Washington, D.C., in the summer of 1950. In 1953, in an X-1A rocket plane, Yeager established a new world speed record of 1,650 mph—twice the speed of sound. By the time the flyboy retired in 1975, he had logged 10,000 hours in 180 different aircraft.

Owing to circumstances—age, bureaucracy—beyond his control, he never did become an astronaut. He never did the ticker tape deal, he never made the cover of LIFE. But that's O.K. It's hard to picture Yeager in a NASA cockpit, with somebody on the ground calling the shots. When he was aloft, he wanted his fate in his own strong hands.

No More Monkey Business

In the space race, **Yuri Gagarin** put
the Soviet Union squarely in the lead.

For centuries, mankind sat around wondering about outer space—"the heavens"—then for decades lolled about wondering what it might be like to travel through space. And then, in the 1950s, it got down to serious business. When mankind stopped wondering and lolling, it assaulted space with a frenzy, not least because the world's two superpowers, the United States and the Soviet Union, felt there were strategic and psychological advantages in getting there ahead of the other. When the U.S.S.R. drew first blood by launching its Sputnik satellite in 1957, the question became: What's next? The answer to that was another question: Which nation will be the first to put a man in space, not to mention bring him back alive?

By 1961 the Soviet and American space programs had blasted seeds, eggs, rats, dogs and a chimpanzee named Ham into space. Some of these guinea pigs—well, actually, there were no guinea pigs—burned up upon reentry into the earth's atmosphere. Some, however, did not: Chernushka and Zvezdochka, two Russian dogs launched into orbit in March aboard Cosmic Ships 4 and 5, respectively, came back yapping. Rumors flew that a man was on deck for the Soviets, and, sure enough, on April 12, 1961, Soviet citizen pilot Lt. Yuri Alekseyevich Gagarin, a choice approved by Premier Nikita Sergeyevich Khrushchev, lifted off.

Gagarin was like many another aviation adventurer—the Wrights, Lindbergh—in that, as a youth, he dreamed of going up, up and away. Born in 1934 on a collective farm, Gagarin was studying metalworking at a school outside Moscow when he joined

GLORY! read the poster celebrating four Vostok missions, and Gagarin was a most glorious idol. He was made a Hero of the Soviet Union, and when he died in 1968, his ashes were buried in the Kremlin Wall. Since then, there have been Elvis-like sightings of the charismatic cosmonaut throughout Russia.

Everett Collection

Gagarin conferred with his mentor, legendary Soviet rocket scientist Sergei Korolev, principal designer of the *Vostok*. Late in Gagarin's flight, the capsule began to gyrate when an umbilical cable didn't release. Mission Control reacted violently: "Malfunction! . . . Don't panic!" Gagarin didn't, though he nearly blacked out. After 10 minutes in the spin cycle, the cable broke.

his first flying club. He enrolled at the Soviet Air Force Academy, graduating with honors in 1957. He became part of the Soviet cosmonaut program, a gang of aviators resembling NASA's storied Mercury 7 team. As the eggs and animals were being shot into space, none of the Soviet fliers knew which of them might be the human test case.

Just four days before the historic launch, Gagarin, 27, learned he was the one. Things started moving very fast: checks, checks, double checks. Gagarin stayed cool. As they closed the door to his cockpit, he was whistling a happy tune.

Gagarin spent 108 minutes in the 9,750-pound *Vostok 1,* orbiting the earth once and flying weightless for 89 minutes. Floating between 112 and 155 miles above the planet, he offered decidedly nonscientific reports—"I can see clouds. I can see everything. It is beautiful!"—in a gaga voice that would be echoed in Soviet and NASA space triumphs to come. Yes, the conquest of space was, on paper, about technological advance. But space was awesome, and those who went there were transformed into wide-eyed adventurers, if not poets.

Gagarin proved that man could withstand a G-force of 7.7 as his spaceship crashed back through the earth's atmosphere. The *Vostok*—Russian for "East"—landed among cows and peasants near the Volga River. Gagarin wasn't aboard. The cosmonaut had jumped ship four miles above ground, floating to safety with a parachute.

Seven years after his history-making rocket ride, Gagarin was killed while piloting a jet.

The First Woman in Space

It was while working in a textile factory in 1961 that 24-year-old Valentina Tereshkova, an amateur parachutist, applied to the Russian cosmonaut program. One of five Russian women trained by Gagarin, Tereshkova proved her mettle, and on June 16, 1963, she lifted off in *Vostok 6.* In 70 hours, 50 minutes, she circled the globe 48 times, spending more time in orbit than all the U.S. Mercury astronauts combined. She traveled 1.2 million miles.

Back on the planet, Tereshkova went on to become president of the Soviet Women's Committee and a member of the U.S.S.R.'s Supreme Soviet. For all her heroism and achievement, her country nevertheless abandoned its special female cosmonaut program and didn't send another woman up until 1982. The U.S. was even slower: Sally Ride didn't travel in the shuttle until 1983.

Sovfoto/Eastfoto

John Launois/Black Star

One reason Tereshkova was chosen for the cosmonaut corps was that she was pretty and would project a positive image. After her '63 flight, she was ready for her closeup.

Ralph Morse (4)

To the Moon and Beyond

In 1969, **Neil Armstrong** and **Buzz Aldrin** proved there were new worlds to conquer.

The risks were otherworldly. If the engine designed to launch the men failed, they would crash. If the engine designed to lift them out of the moon's orbit failed, they would be forever lost in space. If the engine designed to return them to Earth failed, they would burn to death. There were solar and cosmic radiation to worry about, micrometeorites, lunar gravitational fields and whatever surprises the mysterious vacuum that is space might contain.

Eight years earlier—many moons ago—the space program had begun in earnest: Alan Shepard chased Gagarin, becoming the first American in space; John Glenn orbited, becoming the first American to do that; President John F. Kennedy made a new promise, that America would put a man on the lunar surface before decade's end; and the Mercury

Armstrong waved as he led Aldrin and Collins to the command module atop NASA's 6.5-million-pound rocket. The countdown proceeded without incident, and at exactly 9:32 a.m. EDT, 7.5 million pounds of thrust sent the trio hurtling heavenward.

NASA

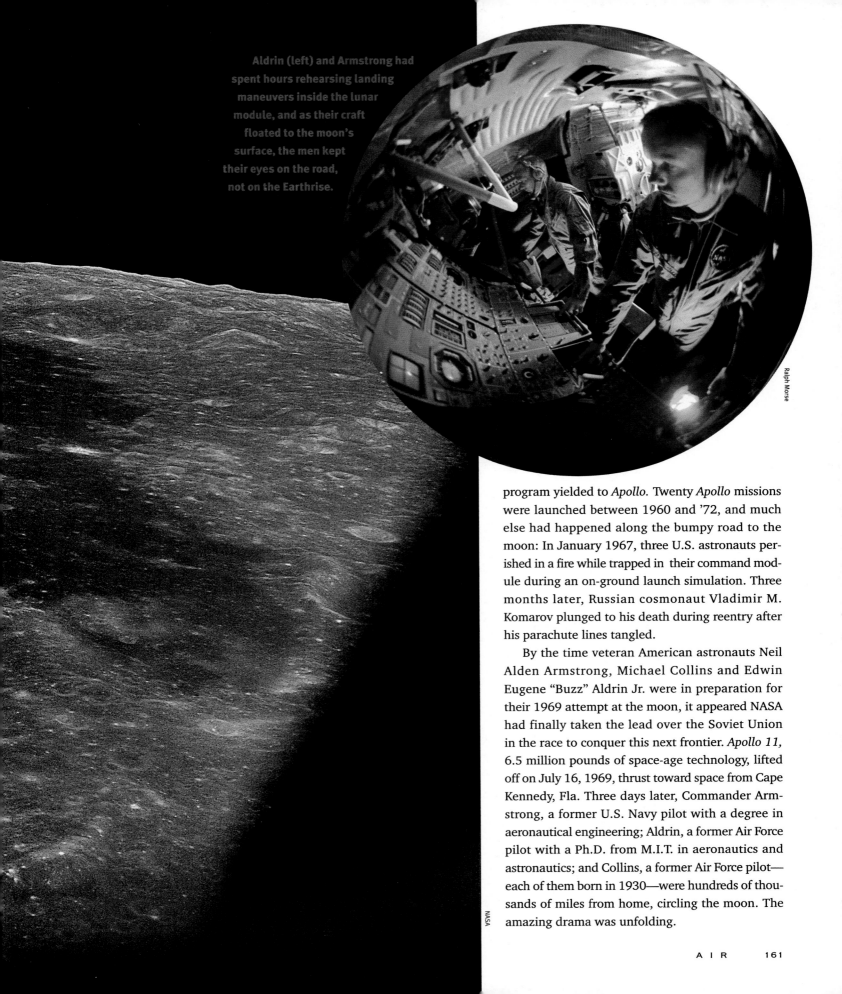

Aldrin (left) and Armstrong had spent hours rehearsing landing maneuvers inside the lunar module, and as their craft floated to the moon's surface, the men kept their eyes on the road, not on the Earthrise.

Ralph Morse

NASA

program yielded to *Apollo.* Twenty *Apollo* missions were launched between 1960 and '72, and much else had happened along the bumpy road to the moon: In January 1967, three U.S. astronauts perished in a fire while trapped in their command module during an on-ground launch simulation. Three months later, Russian cosmonaut Vladimir M. Komarov plunged to his death during reentry after his parachute lines tangled.

By the time veteran American astronauts Neil Alden Armstrong, Michael Collins and Edwin Eugene "Buzz" Aldrin Jr. were in preparation for their 1969 attempt at the moon, it appeared NASA had finally taken the lead over the Soviet Union in the race to conquer this next frontier. *Apollo 11,* 6.5 million pounds of space-age technology, lifted off on July 16, 1969, thrust toward space from Cape Kennedy, Fla. Three days later, Commander Armstrong, a former U.S. Navy pilot with a degree in aeronautical engineering; Aldrin, a former Air Force pilot with a Ph.D. from M.I.T. in aeronautics and astronautics; and Collins, a former Air Force pilot—each of them born in 1930—were hundreds of thousands of miles from home, circling the moon. The amazing drama was unfolding.

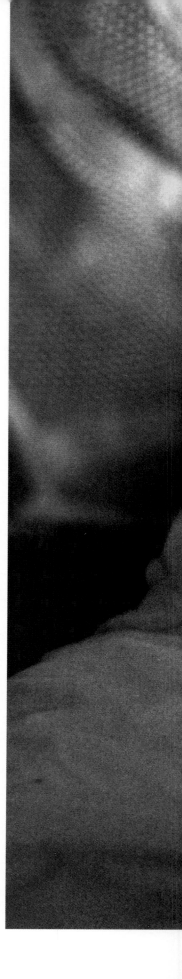

Armstrong performed his one small step nimbly (left), his tasks on the lunar surface ably and his return to the command module smartly. Then, the dramatic adventure over, he allowed himself a smile.

Armstrong and Aldrin climbed aboard the lunar module they had named the *Eagle*. Their compartment was nine feet high, 13 feet wide and 14 feet long and, besides its communication center, contained nothing more than the men, a guidance computer and some food and water. This wasn't really about scientific inquiry, this was about getting there: The *Eagle* had been designed for lunar landing, lunar liftoff and ultimate rendezvous with the command and service module, manned by Collins during his teammates' absence.

On Sunday, July 20, the lunar module broke from the CSM. "The *Eagle* has wings," Armstrong said as he and Aldrin started to make their way the 69 miles to the landing site. Suddenly, Armstrong saw below him a "football-field-sized crater with a large number of big boulders and rocks." He seized the manual controls and piloted the ship to safety, touching down on the intended target, the promisingly named Sea of Tranquility. After reporting the necessary technical information, Armstrong spoke the second of three phrases that still echo all these years later: "Houston, Tranquility base here, the *Eagle* has landed."

A world watched rapt as shadowy images, beamed back through space, seemed to show a man descending a short ladder and stepping onto the moon. What did he say? Did you hear what he said? What Armstrong said—"That's one small step for a man, one giant leap for mankind"—seemed perfect at the time, even if scientists, philosophers and the man in the street would debate in the years ahead how, precisely, getting to the moon represented a leap for mankind.

In any event, the *Eagle*'s two-man crew went on to perform each of its duties on the lunar surface without surprise or malfunction. Toddling along in space suits built to withstand temperatures from minus 250° F to 250° above, as well as any micrometeorites that might be zipping about, Armstrong and Aldrin collected 50 pounds of rock and soil samples. They set up a seismometer to measure earthquakelike activity, a reflector to pick up moon-bound laser beams sent from Earth to measure the exact

Aldrin (above) and Armstrong took many small steps on the moon. Giant leaps were taken by five later *Apollo* missions, all of which deposited astronauts on the spheroid. But man hasn't set foot on the dusty surface since 1972.

distance (turns out, 239,000 miles), and a sheet of foil to trap gases for study back at home. Armstrong and Aldrin spent two hours and 31 minutes walking on the moon before they clambered back into the *Eagle,* which lifted off serenely and rejoined the mother ship.

For the next three days, they and Collins cruised "right down U.S. 1," as Armstrong put it. "Very smooth, very quiet ride." On July 24, 1969, after crashing through Earth's atmosphere at some 25,000 miles an hour, generating temperatures nearing 4000° F, they splashed down in the Pacific, 15 miles from the recovery ship. They were entirely surrounded by a world in awe.

That wasn't the end of it, of course. The saga of *Apollo 13,* marooned in space before being dramatically reeled back to Earth, would follow in 1970. In 1972 the *Apollo* program would close up shop; the final tab would come to $20.4 billion. NASA's recyclable-craft shuttle program would be marked by a string of glorious successes—a cosmic fix-it operation for broken satellites, a taxi to the space stations—and the horrifying tragedy of the *Challenger* explosion in 1986. The Hubble telescope would probe deep space, and Pathfinder would find the surface of Mars. But all these years later, one space adventure still seems magical. Do you believe we put a man on the moon?

Ride didn't dream of being Neil Armstrong when she was an 18-year-old in 1969—it just wasn't on the dream radar of any teenage girl. By the time she caught a catnap on the shuttle in 1983, stars and moonbeams were dancing in her head.

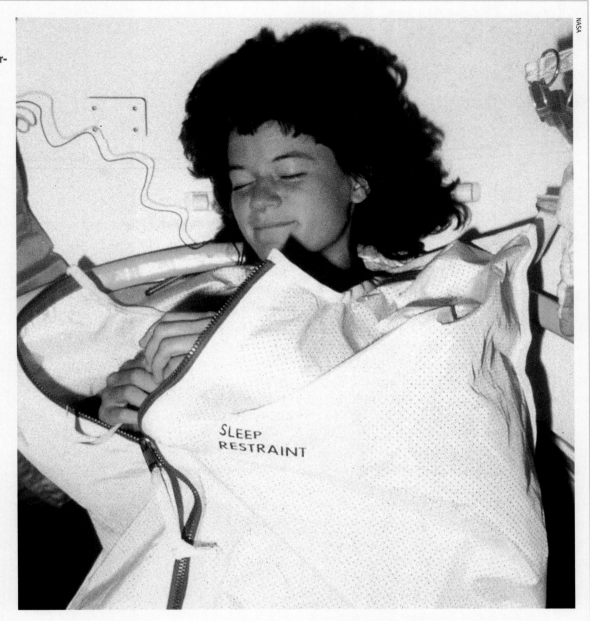

SLEEP RESTRAINT

The Women's Movement

"When I was growing up," wrote Sally Ride in her 1986 autobiography, "I was always fascinated by the planets, stars, and galaxies, but I never thought about becoming an astronaut." Then, as a student finishing up her Ph.D. in physics at Stanford in 1978, she saw an ad in the school paper: NASA was looking for young scientists to serve as mission specialists on its shuttle flights. That sounded pretty exciting.

Of 8,000 applicants, 35, including Ride, were selected; she was one of six women. She performed commendably in training, then waited her turn. On June 18, 1983, twenty-two years after the first U.S. manned space mission, 32-year-old Sally Ride lifted off in the *Challenger* and became the first American woman in space. The six-day mission was partly to test robotics for releasing and retrieving satellites, but, wrote Ride, "the thing that I'll remember most about the flight is that it was fun. In fact, I'm sure it was the most fun I'll ever have in my life."

Many women have followed Ride's pioneering lead, and today any given shuttle-flight staff or space-station roster may well include a woman. A sad footnote: Perhaps the most famous American astronaut since Armstrong and Aldrin remains Christa McAuliffe, the New Hampshire schoolteacher who was chosen to be the first private citizen in space. In 1986, McAuliffe was killed when the *Challenger*—the same ship that had carried Sally Ride—exploded shortly after liftoff.

Man Versus Myth

In a pedal-powered aircraft,
Kanellos Kanellopoulos chased
a record—and a legend.

Daedalus was persecuted by King Minos, the story has it, and he wanted to get out of Dodge—or, at least, Knossos. Good for him that he was a craftsman. He built wings of feather, wax and thread, and strapped them on. He flapped mightily, lifted off and flew across the sea to freedom.

Unlikely descendants of Daedalus turned up at the Massachusetts Institute of Technology, where, in the late 1980s, a team of students and professors decided they would mimic the mythic escape. If they were able to cross the Aegean, they would, in the bargain, shatter the world distance record for human-powered flight set in 1979 when the pedal-powered *Gossamer Albatross* floated 22 miles across the English Channel. The M.I.T. craft, named *Daedalus 88,* was constructed of balsa, graphite tubing and Styrofoam and featured a cockpit of Kevlar 1/100th-inch thick. Without burdensome feathers, it came in at a lean 70 pounds. Now all that was needed was a source to provide one third horsepower of energy for four consecutive hours.

Enter Greek Olympic cyclist Kanellos Kanellopoulos. On April 23, 1988, he started pedaling furiously at one end of a runway on the island of Crete. His heartbeat was 150 per minute before the craft even lifted off. Kanellopoulos kept up the effort—likened to running back-to-back marathons—for three hours and 54 minutes. Sipping an energizing cocktail of sugar, water and salt as he went, Kanellopoulos glided 30 feet above the calm sea. Just a tantalizing 10 yards from the island of Santorini, a headwind hit. The fragile wings folded, the tail snapped and Kanellopoulos plunged into the water. Unhurt, he swam to shore and emerged exultant. *Daedalus* had flown 72.4 miles and had set three world records for human-powered flight— the most miles flown in one flight, the longest flight in a straight line and the most time spent aloft.

Kanellopoulos was chosen to pilot *Daedalus* on its historic flight (right) after a sort of mini–Mercury 7 training program. Hundreds of aspirants had bid for the job, and five elite athletes were tapped to train as fliers. Kanellopoulos and the others rode bikes up to 400 miles a week under the watchful eye of project manager John S. Langford and his M.I.T. colleagues. Ultimately, Kanellopoulos was the man to replicate what Langford grandly called, "the first chapter of nearly every anthology of flight."

Chuck O'Rear/Woodfin Camp

A Couple of Voyagers

Dick Rutan and **Jeana Yeager** took a nonstop, round-the-world flight of fancy—and daring.

They were just 1,200 miles short of the goal when air bubbles caused a fuel pump to malfunction, which made the rear engine sputter and quit. "Now we've lost it," Dick Rutan said to his copilot and girlfriend, Jeana Yeager. The airplane *Voyager* began to dive from 8,000 feet. Rutan and Yeager tried to restart the engine. In minutes, the plane would crash into the Pacific Ocean off Baja California.

Let's leave them there for just a moment.

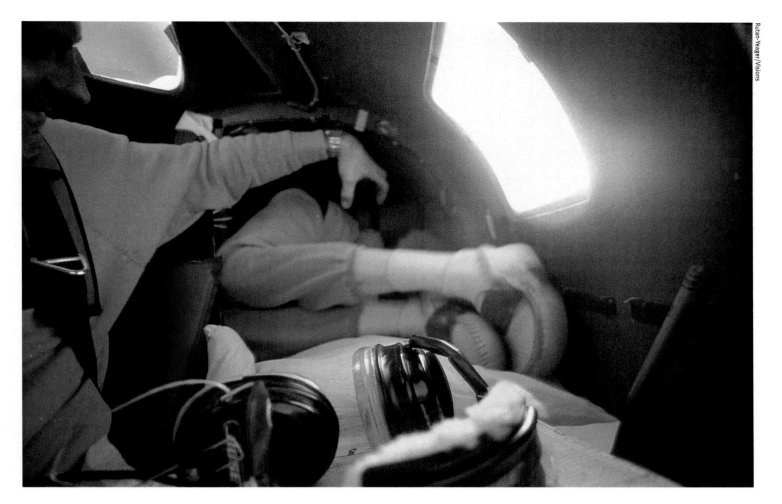

Rutan-Yeager/Visions

In a cockpit the size of a telephone booth, Yeager caught catnaps when she could (above). Eventually, both pilots were exhausted by more than a week aloft. "One minute I was fine," said Rutan, "and the next minute I couldn't remember how to do anything." His brother summed up: "Obviously, this flight was not insured."

"If it were easy, it would have been done before," Yeager—no relation to Chuck—said in 1986 of circling the earth in a plane: 25,012 miles, nonstop on its own supply of gas. The first global circumnavigation, in 1924, took 175 days, 61 stops, 30 spare engines and fuel donated by 28 countries. The first nonstop loop, by the U.S. Air Force in 1949, required four refueling rendezvous. A big plane needed too much fuel, and a small plane couldn't carry enough.

The lightweight *Voyager* was neither big nor small. Constructed of plastics, paper and epoxy, it weighed 1,858 pounds empty but could tote 7,394 pounds of fuel—80 percent of its total weight—plus pilots and equipment. It was built for the long haul, certainly not for comfort. "Even the slightest bit of turbulence makes the aircraft bounce as if you were in rough seas in a rowboat," said Burt Rutan, Dick's brother and the plane's designer.

The strange craft took off—barely—on December 14, 1986, from Edwards Air Force Base outside Los Angeles. With flexible wings burdened by 1,320 gallons of fuel, the plane scraped its wingtips as it struggled down the 15,000-foot runway, finally lifting off with just 1,000 feet left. "Technically, we should have aborted," said Dick Rutan.

Averaging 115 mph, *Voyager* soared over Southeast Asia, the Indian Ocean and Africa, where Yeager and Rutan, bringing the plane up to 20,000 feet, donned oxygen masks. The altitude was still too much for Yeager, who suffered hypoxia and blacked out. She was revived by the time *Voyager,* at lower altitude, zoomed over the Atlantic. A storm flipped the plane onto its side, but Rutan regained control.

With the end in sight, that rear engine went and the plane headed down. And then . . .

"Why don't you start the front engine?" radioed Mike Melvill from *Voyager*'s mission control. What a good idea! The pilots flicked switches, and at 3,500 feet the front engine caught and the plane leveled off, enabling fuel to reach the back engine, restarting it. On December 23, nine days, three minutes and 44 seconds after takeoff, *Voyager* touched down at Edwards, a day early and with a mere 18 gallons of fuel to spare.

The Adventurer of Tomorrow

In 1997, a robot named **Sojourner** sailed the heavens.

Think of Pathfinder as the dogsled and Sojourner (right) as Peary. Think of Mars as the North Pole: a cold, barren, inhospitable realm. As was the case in Peary's day, there were those who considered it silly to spend so much time and money reaching such a place. But, as in Peary's day—indeed, as ever—there were millions more who were thrilled once the place was reached.

We felt we were with him. The "him" was NASA's Sojourner, an anthropomorphized representative of the human race that, riding a rocket named Pathfinder, transported us 310 million miles to Mars in 1997. Pathfinder's voyage had lasted seven months; on July 4, it took us minutes to tune in as the 25-pound skateboard-size robot maneuvered over the Martian landscape looking for signs of life, of water, of anything interesting. Sojourner beamed back images of salmon skies and red rock canyons, strikingly like Ray Bradbury's imaginings in his classic *The Martian Chronicles.* Sojourner brought back chemical analyses of rock that proved Mars was, at some point, more Earth-like than scientists had believed. Sojourner did its job well. Dare we say, nobly? Bravely?

Men may still go to Mars; some NASA officials are hoping this will happen within the next two decades. But certainly the robot made a giant leap into the future of exploration and adventuring. Realize this: We would not yet have reached Mars if we hadn't gone this way. We don't have an ironclad solution for exposure to cosmic rays found beyond Earth's protective magnetic zone, and the National Research Council reports that the "increased lifetime risk of cancer" for astronauts journeying to Mars "could be as high as 40 percent." Moreover, a manned mission is exponentially more costly than a robotic mission because of support and safety measures that must be built in.

Does technology make adventuring a bloodless, unexciting sport? To a degree it does, surely. But then we look at the reaction engendered by Sojourner among earthlings—cheers when its ship touched down, a sense of awe and wonder at its images, a tingle—and we say: "Quite an adventure."

NASA

Nothing Left Undone

Shortly after liftoff, the *Orbiter 3* was captured against the panorama of the Swiss Alps, coated in winter snow. After nearly three weeks alone together, Piccard (left) and Jones were still fast friends.

Denis Balibouse/Reuters/Archive Pictures

Closing out a century of adventure, balloonists **Bertrand Piccard** and **Brian Jones** went around the world in 20 days.

On March 1, 1999, the morning of his 41st birthday, Bertrand Piccard of Switzerland awoke and vomited. He hadn't been out carousing the night before; in fact, he had turned in early, knowing he had to be up-and-at-'em for a rendezvous at a designated field in the Swiss Alps. There, awaiting him, would be thousands of countrymen and an 18-story balloon named the *Breitling Orbiter 3*—the sources of Piccard's queasiness.

"If only these people knew how frightened we are inside!" he said as he gazed at the crowd. Piccard's partner in fear was his copilot, Brian Jones, an Englishman. The two men, their balloon and an extensive team were engaged in a fevered, big-money race to knock off what looked like the last pure Jules Verne–type adventure available: to go around the planet nonstop in a hot-air balloon. The race to

Fabrice Coffrini/Keystone/AFP

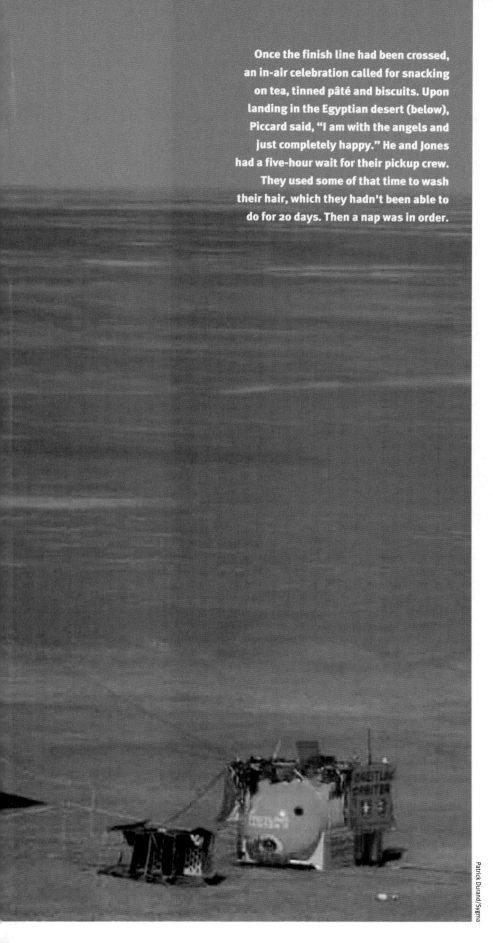

Once the finish line had been crossed, an in-air celebration called for snacking on tea, tinned pâté and biscuits. Upon landing in the Egyptian desert (below), Piccard said, "I am with the angels and just completely happy." He and Jones had a five-hour wait for their pickup crew. They used some of that time to wash their hair, which they hadn't been able to do for 20 days. Then a nap was in order.

be first to do this extraordinary thing had spurred 21 attempts since 1981 and had lured an extraordinary cast of competitors to the fray. Most famously, British media billionaire Richard Branson launched high-tech efforts three times in 1997–98, and American multimillionaire securities-broker-cum-thrill-seeker Steve Fossett became, during his 1998 try, the first person to cross the Pacific in a balloon, solo.

Piccard had tried twice before and therefore had no certainty in 1999 that he would succeed. Things got off poorly when, during the final pre-liftoff preparations, the balloon, still tethered, was lifted six feet up, then slammed back down with a thunderous crash. But it finally took flight, at 9:05 a.m., in gusty winds, as the crowd cheered. Below, in the village of Château-d'Oex, church bells rang out.

Jones and Piccard spent the next 20 days sealed in a pressurized 18-by-10-foot capsule, surrounded by 32 tanks of fuel and held aloft by helium, hot air and propane. They faced not only unpredictable weather but flight restrictions over China. To steer a course, Jones, a ballooning instructor, and Piccard, a psychiatrist and the son of Jacques, the Marianas Trench bathyscaph pilot, increased and decreased their altitude to catch wind currents. They climbed as high as 36,000 feet, into temperatures as low as –62°F. At one point, 300 pounds of ice formed on the balloon. They descended to 10,000 feet, and Piccard climbed through the capsule's hatch. With a fire ax he chipped off 10-foot icicles.

By and large, jet streams worked their magic— "the most striking fact about the whole flight was that we had such extraordinary luck," said Piccard— and they zipped over Europe, Africa, Asia and the Pacific. They lost the stream over Mexico and, during a half-day detour, drifted south toward Venezuela. Then they got back on the highway and flew across Central America, the Atlantic and into Africa. On March 20, the *Breitling Orbiter 3* crossed its finish line, over Mauritania, but Piccard and Jones kept going until, several hours later, they touched down in a remote part of the Egyptian desert. They had flown 19 days, 21 hours and 55 minutes, covered 29,018 miles and set world records for distance and duration. Piccard recalled their moment of victory: "We stood up and embraced, shaking hands, slapping each other on the back, and shouting, 'It's incredible. We've done it! We've done it!'"

Summit Meeting

In the Golden Age of Adventuring, they were rivals, if rarely dinner companions. But the titans of polar exploration—from left, the Irishman Ernest Shackleton, the American Robert E. Peary and the Norwegian Roald Amundsen—did have occasion to break bread. In January 1913 the sponsors of an Amundsen lecture in Philadelphia thought it would be a good idea "to have the discoverer of the North Pole introduce the discoverer of the South Pole." Peary agreed to share the dais. Shackleton had recently been pleased to hear flattery floated his way by Amundsen, and he showed up too and said a few words. He didn't miss the chance to thank Amundsen publicly for being "good enough to say that I blazed the way for him." All was very decorous, but whatever backstage gossip was shared—belittling Vasco da Gama and Balboa, perhaps?—is lost to history.

From Buenos Aires, Argentina

Rescue Mission

Elephant Island

South Georgia Island

Patience Camp

ATLANTIC OCEAN

Seal Nunataks

PACIFIC OCEAN

Ocean Camp

Endurance Sinks

WEDDELL SEA

RONNE ICE SHELF

Endurance Trapped

Shackleton's Expedition, 1914–16

Byrd's Little America, 1929

Byrd's Flight, 1929

Amundsen's Expedition, 1911–12

South Pole

Bay of Whales

ROSS ICE SHELF

ROSS SEA

Ross Island

Scott's Expedition, 1911–12

ANTARCTICA

Scott's Party Dies on Return Journey

Steger's Expedition, 1989–90

INDIAN OCEAN

Mirnyy